The Seven Life Processes

UNDERSTANDING AND SUPPORTING THEM IN HOME, KINDERGARTEN AND SCHOOL

Philipp Gelitz and Almuth Strehlow

Translated from the German by Nina Kuettel

WECAN
WALDORF EARLY CHILDHOOD
ASSOCIATION OF NORTH AMERICA

The Seven Life Processes:
Understanding and Supporting Them in Home, Kindergarten, and School
First English Edition
© 2016 Waldorf Early Childhood Association of North America
ISBN: 978-1-936849-34-5

First published in German in 2014 by Verlag Freies Geistesleben
as *Die sieben Lebensprozesse: Grundlagen und pädagogische Bedeutung*
in Elternhaus, Kindergarten und Schule

English Edition Editorial Consultant: Susan Howard
Translation: Nina Kuettel
Copy Editing and Graphic Design: Lory Widmer
Proofreading: Bill Day

This publication was made possible
by a grant from the Waldorf Curriculum Fund.

Waldorf Early Childhood Association of North America
285 Hungry Hollow Rd.
Spring Valley, NY 10977
845-352-1690
info@waldorfearlychildhood.org
www.waldorfearlychildhood.org

For a complete book catalog, contact WECAN or visit our online store:
store.waldorfearlychildhood.org

Contents

In olden times
There lived in the souls of initiates
Powerfully the thought
That by nature
Every person is ill.
And education was seen
As a healing process
Which gave the child, as he matured
The health to be a true human being.

Es war in alten Zeiten,
Da lebte in der Eingeweihten Seelen
Kraftvoll der Gedanke, dass krank
Von Natur ein jeglicher Mensch sei.
Und Erziehen ward angesehen
Gleich dem Heilprozess,
Der dem Kinde mit dem Reifen
Die Gesundheit zugleich erbrachte
Für des Lebens vollendetes Menschsein.

NOTE: This verse is found in a circular dated March 11, 1924, sent from the Goetheanum to medical people and signed by Rudolf Steiner and Ita Wegman. It was published as part of the *Course for Young Doctors*, GA 316. This translation is taken from the 2006 Kolisko conference program.

Preface

In the daily practice of Waldorf education — in kindergarten, school, child care settings, and curative education, but also in the areas of social therapy and adult education — we carry an image of the human being into our work as the basis for our actions. Depending on one's field of expertise, one person becomes expert in a certain subject and the next is well-versed in another area. In the field of anthroposophical education the one unifying factor is the internalized knowledge of a human being's four "bodies." Through Rudolf Steiner's spiritual-scientific research we know about the structure of the human organism as it is manifested on Earth today in the form of physical body, etheric (or life) body, astral body and ego body (or "I"). Daily contact with the expressions of the physical and life bodies, of feelings and perceptions, and of "I" individualities supports this knowledge to quite an impressive degree.

A deeper look into the interrelationships of functions in the etheric or life body brings to light a mysterious connection. The living forces we use to preserve and regenerate our physical body, always protecting it from decay — that is, the formative forces that integrate physical matter into life functions — are the same forces we use to develop our faculties of imagination, thought, and memory. This has to do with a primal developmental phenomenon unique to humankind; namely, the transformation of etheric formative forces into mental or soul faculties.

Our aim is to precisely illuminate this transformation by highlighting a very specific aspect of the etheric: the seven life processes. There are many perspectives from which it would be worthwhile to investigate the etheric; the seven life processes constitute one of these. A study of the life processes can help us acquire a concrete view of the etheric and its forms of expression.

This study also allows for the possibility of gaining a clearer understanding of what "the birth of the etheric body," a phrase often used in anthroposophy (see the section on "Metamorphosis of Etheric Formative Forces"), actually means, and of the sophisticated and nuanced manner in which the transformation of etheric forces takes place.

This book was written for parents, teachers, and caregivers alike. Regardless of any specific pedagogical task you may have, occupying yourself with the subject of the life processes can shed light on your own learning behavior and approach to the world as an adult.

Rudolf Steiner provided some basic thoughts about the life processes in just two places in his extensive legacy. In the seventh lecture of the series *The Riddle of Humanity* (GA 170), he describes the connection between the seven life processes and the twelve senses. In the unfinished work *Anthroposophy (A Fragment)* (GA 45), he virtually calls on us to do further research.

Several authors have already done admirable work in elucidating the life processes and how they are interconnected, especially Coenraad van Houten in his book *Awakening the Will: Principles and Processes in Adult Learning,* regarding one's own learning behavior, as well as Christof Lindenau in his work *Der übende Mensch,* on the subject of self-education. In some instances, these books may attribute different soul faculties to different individual life processes than are suggested in the following pages. This does not mean that any of the classifications are wrong, misguided, or incomplete. Rather, the problem occurs because the life processes and the soul faculties that develop from them "flow in and out and on top of each other," as Rudolf Steiner put it. They do not appear separately from one another. For this reason, when looked at from various perspectives, in each case something different, or differently characterized, can step into the foreground of an observation without inferring error on the part of another. The *effort* to characterize the relationship of the living substructure to the soul-spirit aspect will be the decisive factor, as opposed to "one correct" conceptual framework.

In addition, a fundamental examination of the relationship of the seven life processes to the twelve senses was given to us by Karl König in his book, *A Living Physiology,* with very insightful discoveries for curative education. Likewise for Benita Quadflieg-von Vegesack's book, *Ungewöhnliche Kleinkinder und ihre heilpädagogische Förderung,* although this book is not available in English. However, until now, the seven life processes have never been the central focus of study, even though in anthroposophy they are the starting point for an understanding of that which is physically alive and of the non-physical soul-spirit aspect. In Hermann Pfrogner's book, *Die sieben Lebensprozesse, Eine musiktherapeutische Anregung*, the topic has been researched specifically for music therapists.

The intention of this book is to *approach and draw near to* the phenomenon of that which is physically alive from the viewpoint of the seven life processes, so that the living substructure, with its rhythmic and functional principles, upon which all education and self-education should be based, will advance further into awareness. Consequently, the seven life processes, described by Rudolf Steiner for the first time in 1910, also constitute an area of life science that, along with natural science, is urgently needed for understanding the basic principles of the free development of the soul and spirit.

Philipp Gelitz and Almuth Strehlow
Kassel, Germany 2013

On the Trail of Living Substances

If we take a handful of earth, we have in our hand a multiplicity of the most varied microorganisms. Every tiny little bit of soil is teeming with life. However, from a physical standpoint, every animal, plant and human being consists merely of carbon, hydrogen and oxygen, along with a few other chemical elements. What is it that allows a living organism to develop from these material elements?

When a seed is put in the ground, placing it in connection with soil, water, air, and light over a period of days and weeks, roots develop. These in turn release mineral substances in the soil from their existing chemical bonds, making them available to the germinating plant. The peculiar thing is that now these mineral substances form chemical bonds that never previously occurred in the soil. They form new chemical bonds in the soil *only* when a living organism absorbs them; either via roots, as with plants, or via nourishment, as with animals. Setting aside the microbial life streaming through it, different chemical principles hold sway in the soil than in life forms.

Certainly, there are chemical processes taking place in non-living matter, but they are completely different from those in living matter. Not only are there isolated carbon, oxygen, or sodium atoms in the soil, but also unique chemical bonds that produce quartz, amethyst, and all the other mineral forms we so admire. The energy created by these mineral forms is a subject worthy of another book; *however, the underlying principles are completely different.* A special characteristic of living matter is its ability to bring mineral substances into new chemical bonds that could never form without this living element. Thus, there has to be a force that is able to surmount the principles of the mineral element in order to create something new from it.

Mineral forms are crystalline in nature. There are certain organizational principles and forms of deposits and salt formations that can be observed. If a living organism comes upon these mineral forms and absorbs them, either through its roots, like plants, or through a process of nourishment, like animals and human beings, the living organism brings the elements of the mineral forms into a new relationship. However, the new chemical bond is not the only remarkable aspect. What is even more amazing is that the mineral substance is brought to a higher level in the truest sense of the word.

That is to say, in the mineral kingdom the law of gravity is at work, but in living matter it is the law of levity, or buoyancy. When a plant's roots free mineral elements from the soil, they stream upward through the plant's system of liquid absorption and distribution. The law of gravity has obviously been surmounted. The most visible element in living matter is water, and in it substances that were once mineral are transformed into living matter. It is within the watery element that the living element in plants, animals and human beings forms sugar, starch, cellulose, protein, and fat from mineral substances. Where before only certain formations could appear in the mineral element, in the living element a formative force can be observed that surmounts the laws of the mineral element and, through new bonds of matter, leads to completely new forms and even to vital functions such as maintaining, growing, or reproducing. A rose quartz crystal cannot reproduce; it forms through a necessity of the environment, with its various substances and conditions of pressure and heat. (From an anthroposophical viewpoint, the fact that these exact substances are present, along with the necessary conditions of pressure and heat, is considered the interplay of cosmic forces and elemental beings working in the Earth. However, the influence of these forces will not be elaborated upon further here.) In contrast, an oak tree does not develop out of a necessity of the environment, but because a living, driving impulse to propagate causes the tree to form acorns. Such an acorn falls to the ground and through its internal, living, formative force, and with the help of water, air, and light, earth substances are transformed and a new tree develops.

But what is it that allows a living organism to develop? A living organism does not just develop from material found in the mineral world; it is already present as an idea, a thought in the cosmos. The thought can embody itself as a living form if a seed is put in the ground. Then the life force of the embodying idea can surmount the laws of the mineral element and subordinate them to its own formative impulse. It is especially impressive to observe this after seeds lying dormant for years in dry, desert sands are "awakened" all at once by an infrequent rain. In this case, through the element of water, suddenly the right conditions are produced for the gorgeous, colorful embodiment of different formative ideas; conditions not there previously. But regardless of that, the idea of a specific kind of plant already existed, only it could not show itself as a living organism at this particular spot. Formative impulses and living functions do not develop; they *embody* themselves when the right conditions are present. This also applies to organ formation in both animals and humans.

If we turn our attention to human beings, it is clear that the life pulsing through a human being looks very different from that of a plant. Under the influence of the astral aspect, completely different facets of the etheric show themselves in the breathing process, the system of taking in nourishment, the digestive process, warmth production, and also the way in which human beings reproduce. A plant does in fact reproduce, but in a different manner than animals and human beings. Plants require a temperature range that allows them to survive. Under a covering of snow in the winter, plants use their system of liquid absorption and distribution to produce a warmer microclimate than the immediate surroundings. However, a plant's ability to produce warmth is less strongly developed than it is in animals and human beings.

Something similar can be observed with the system of taking in nourishment and digestion. A plant absorbs nutrients via its roots and subsequently uses them. However, plants have a different system of digestion than the intestinal activity that takes place in ensouled, living beings and creatures. Wherever there are cavity formations in the body, such as in the lungs, mouth, esophagus and digestive tract, the astral aspect influences the processes and formations of the etheric and physical aspects, as is the case with animals and human beings. Plants orient themselves to these astral influences but they have not assimilated them. From this perspective, plants have the same life processes as humans and animals, but they are less internal in nature. A plant takes in carbon dioxide and gives off oxygen, but instead of using an internal organ, this takes place on the surface of its leaves. Plants send a reproductive impulse up towards light and warmth, but are strongly dependent upon insects and wind in order to propagate successfully. And they nourish themselves through their roots in a much more direct way than the internalized process of the metabolic organ system, consisting of mouth, stomach and intestines, that is found in animals and human beings.

In this respect, what differentiates human beings from animals is the gradual and partial detachment from a purely physical orientation of the life processes. An animal breathes, and in so doing the life process of breathing remains static. It is different with human beings. In the first seven years of life, a human being re-forms the inherited physical body with the help of etheric forces, according to the requirements of the individuality. When this process has reached a certain conclusion, a portion of these etheric forces are released. The remaining forces no longer work to build up and reshape the physical body, but rather, on a physical level, only strive to maintain and regenerate existing forms and functions. Through this process, a part of the etheric formative forces are released which then remain available for activities of the imagination, memory, and intellect for the rest of a person's life. So, a human being does not just breathe as an animal breathes, but rather the life process known as "breathing" becomes increasingly more autonomous in the physical body during the course of childhood so that there is a gradual development of soul faculties; beginning with perception, then attention, and finally, in conjunction with other processes, concentration. The lungs develop and the rhythmic processes stabilize themselves in the circulatory and digestive systems; to the same extent will the etheric formative forces, which accomplish all of this through the life process of breathing, be released.

From this perspective, it becomes clear that animals possess only those etheric forces that are active in human beings purely for the purpose of regeneration. That which goes beyond this, and even provides a human being with the power to reshape the hereditary physical body, is not present in animals. The power of the "I" to individualize body and soul is missing in animals and this has consequences for the etheric body and the possibility of transformation. In the last chapter of this book this aspect will be covered in more detail.

Breathing is only one of the seven life processes. Besides breathing, one also finds the process of warmth production, or *warming*. We have within us a life process that allows us to warm and cool ourselves. It is a process of continuously seeking balance, of putting things into proportion. The ability to produce warmth during physical activity, and regulatory mechanisms such as perspiration in connection with the secretion process, are also related to this. The warming process is most clearly demonstrated by the fact that humans can survive in arctic cold as well as tropical heat. The various organs of the human body live within different temperatures, which illustrates the complexity of this process.

Two more life processes are *nourishing* and *secreting*. These two processes are very closely linked during the ingestion of food. However, close examination reveals a fundamental functional difference between taking in, combining, and disintegrating (nourishing) and sorting, retaining, and excreting (secreting). It is not only in food digestion that these two life processes are found, but also in cell metabolism and the processing of sensory impressions.

The next life process is *maintaining*. This involves the physical organism's ability to constantly maintain its forms and functions, to protect itself against decay. Wound healing is related to the maintaining process.

Further, one is able to observe the life process of *growing*. This is a very critical process, next to breathing, warming, nourishing, secreting and maintaining. If a specific form or function is present, then it also has the possibility of growth. For example, children's fully formed bones are still capable of growth and, likewise, the various organs do not remain the same size they were at birth, but continue to grow without having to relinquish either form or function.

The last life process is *reproducing*. Reproduction processes continually take place in the body when certain physical matter, specific cells or specific organ functions must be produced. The possibility of reproduction after the sexual organs have matured is the most visible result of this life process.

The following section will reveal in detail the seven life processes and their transformations in the human body. Hopefully, it will help us gain a little more understanding of the life that "flows through us," according to Rudolf Steiner, and provide suggestions and encouragement for life with children at home, kindergarten, and school, as well as for one's own self-education.

The Seven Life Processes in Human Beings

There is not just one life force. You have to differentiate; the sense of life, through which we perceive life, is something different from what I am talking about now. I am talking about life itself and how it flows through us; and that is further differentiated within us in the following way... There are no further internal life processes other than these seven. Life is divided into these seven processes... We have:

Breathing
Warming
Nourishing
Secreting
Maintaining
Growing
Reproducing

— Rudolf Steiner, *The Riddle of Humanity* (GA 170)

In several places, Rudolf Steiner mentioned the differentiation of various aspects of life forces; however, he gave an indication of the seven life processes in only two of his works. He spoke of how these processes of life stream through us, or rather, how life "flows through us" (see above). In contrast, there are the static domains of the twelve senses, which are predisposed in the body from out of spiritual impulses; each one within its own defined limits and circumscribed by its associated sense organ. The sense organs' function is to make something known, and the "I" moves freely among them and perceives their manifestations. (See Steiner, *Anthroposophy (A Fragment)*, GA 45.) In contrast, the life processes pulse through these organs, and all other physical structures, in a differentiated way, making possible, as well as maintaining, physical forms and functions. Viewed in this way, the etheric element in human beings, by way of the seven life processes, effects the formation of the physical being, the continual preservation of living functions and, through this, the sense perceptions, which become the foundation upon which the "I" develops its faculty of judgment.

The first time Rudolf Steiner mentioned the seven life processes was in 1910. At that time he was in the process of publishing a book with the title *Anthroposophy*, which, however, was actually published posthumously because Steiner himself never was satisfied that it was the final version. The relationship between the senses and the life processes has an important place in the manuscript and shows how much significance Steiner placed on the seven life processes; they are very important to the relationship of human beings, and all their aspects of being, with the surrounding world. After Steiner's death the manuscript was published under the title: *Anthroposophie. Ein Fragment*. The book offers deep insight into the struggle for living, precisely-defined knowledge of human beings. The fact that in 1910 Steiner was still working under the assumption that there were only ten senses, with the sense of touch and the "I"-sense occupying a special category, is not relevant to our understanding of the seven life processes. However, it does show with what spirit of exploration he struggled to develop his model of the twelve senses, which he was able to complete only after years of research. (By the way, current assumptions about the physiology of the senses are likewise in continual development; today, there is already talk of nine senses; see the Appendix).

Steiner emphasized that there are less clearly defined boundaries between the seven life processes than between the senses, and that they intermingle with one another:

"The sense of taste is, for example, strictly separated from the sense of sight; the life processes are more interrelated; they move in and out of each other to a greater extent. Breathing moves into warming, which moves into nourishing." The life processes feature "organs that flow into one another. The lungs — the primary breathing organ — are connected with the organs of blood circulation, which serve in warmth production; these in turn flow together with the organs of digestion which are connected with nourishing, and so on" (Steiner, *Anthroposophy (A Fragment)*, GA 45).

The following will examine the life processes in detail and explore how they are related to the release of soul faculties.

Breathing

The first sign of life for a newborn human being is the first breath. The rhythmic processes of the developing body are implemented in the mother's womb by connecting with her life processes through the umbilical cord. However, from the placenta onward, the baby's own blood is flowing. With the first breath, tiny lungs begin their own development and a life process that is independent of the mother has begun. Before birth, a baby's blood circulates in a single stream and only with the first breath is arterial blood flow separated from venous blood flow in the heart. At birth the movement of the lungs and the blood circulation begin to correlate with one another and a breath-to-pulse ratio is created.

It is easy to understand why breathing has to be the first recognized life process. Breathing is what allows the implementation of all the other life processes. Without it there can be no warmth production independent of external conditions, since after birth blood circulation is dependent upon breathing. At the same time, breathing is a precondition for warmth production. Since warmth has to be produced at the location of metabolic activity associated with nourishing and secretion, it is a precondition for those two life processes. They, in turn, are preconditions for the maintaining process, and so on.

From the viewpoint of the seven life processes, the breathing process is the basic precondition for human life. If it stops, within a few minutes a person is unable to remain alive. Our states of consciousness are directly connected to the breathing process. While inhaling and exhaling, our soul-spirit aspects (Greek word "pneuma" = air/spirit) oscillate between binding and loosening in a living body.

Upon examining the basic elements that make up the air we breathe, we find interesting number relationships. According to Rudolf Steiner's characterization, something like 78 percent of the air we breathe is nitrogen, which has been barely touched upon in medical research. (See Steiner, *Esoteric Lessons, Part I*, GA 266). About 20 percent is oxygen, which is sent into the bloodstream from the lungs in amounts that vary greatly between individuals. Even the tiniest premature infants (those born in the twenty-fifth week, for example) show the presence of their individuality in this regard, because if the air they breathe has only a fraction too much oxygen content, the corneas may become detached or there could be bleeding in the brain.

Along with oxygen, carbon has been intensively researched, even though the amount of carbon in the air is only something like one-tenth of one percent. We are aware of the connection between carbon and unconsciousness and know about the deadly effects of inhaling too much carbon monoxide. We also know that carbon dioxide is what allows the formation of calcium carbonate in our bones.

Breathing begins immediately after birth; pressure built up in the lungs diminishes and the first exhalation takes place. Blood circulation is now dependent upon breathing because an immediate dependency upon oxygen has been created. At the same time, it is the beginning of the soul's capacity for emotion and perception, because, from now on, there is a constant exchange going on between internal and external aspects — a physical representation of the soul-nature of the human being.

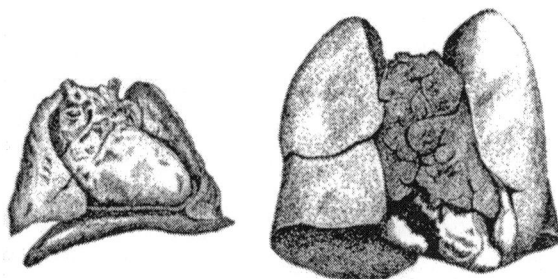

FIGURES 1 AND 2
Left: Infant's heart and lungs.
Right: The lungs of a two-year old. The heart is partially covered by the thymus gland.
Source: Kranich, 1999

At birth the lungs are still very small; not only because the baby is small, for the lungs are small even relative to the size of the baby. The lungs are just able to reach around the little heart one time (see Figure 1). Consequently, the amount of air that can be inhaled is relatively small.

During the course of childhood the lungs grow much longer. By age two the size ratio between heart and lungs already looks very different (see Figure 2). Directly after birth, the volume of air in the lungs is about one liter. Adults have a lung volume of four to six liters (top-performing athletes may have higher lung volume). The so-called total capacity of the lungs is not utilized completely for breathing. While an infant needs an air volume of merely 20 to 50 ml. for breathing, an adult can make do with a volume of 500 ml. As adults we are able to deliberately inhale approximately two to two-and-a-half liters, and exhale approximately one to one-and-a-half liters, in addition to our normal breathing.

Breathing is clearly an unstable process and very changeable in its intensity. Something that is especially demonstrated here is that the kind of breathing determines how the soul-spirit aspect is integrated. The deeper an inhaled breath can branch out into the organism, the greater the experience of one's own "I."

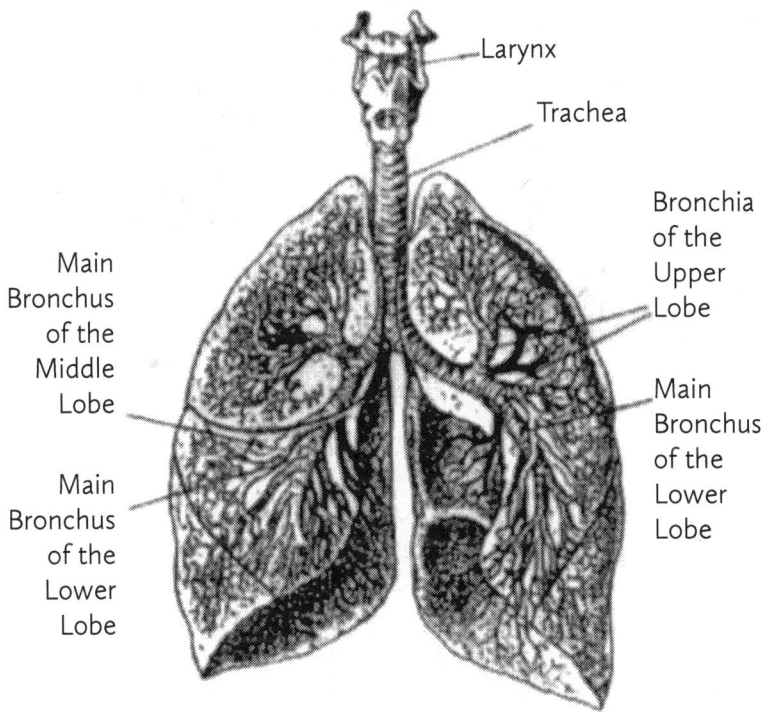

FIGURE 3
Adult lungs, showing larynx, trachea, and bronchial tubes.
Source: http://www2.uni-jena.de/erzwiss/projekte_2004/martin_laudenback_kohl/Anatomie_Lunge.html

There is much less branching in the bronchial area of the lungs in an infant, and many fewer points of contact between breath and blood in the pulmonary alveoli (air sacs) than in a school-age child. The number of air sacs drastically increases during the preschool years, resulting in adult lungs having a very large surface area (approximately 70 to 80 square meters, sometimes more) through which the air is distributed into smaller spaces. The so-called bronchial tree with its trunks and branches that spread out and become smaller and smaller (20 to 23 branches, see Figure 3) is an organ formation that develops rather slowly. At birth it is estimated a baby has "only" one-third the number of air sacs in the lungs as an adult. Adults have an estimated 300 million (!) air sacs.

It is now easy to comprehend Steiner's reference in *The Child's Changing Consciousness as the Basis of Pedagogical Practice* (GA 306) to the fact that first an "adequate ratio" of breath to pulse has to be created as a physical basis for experiencing the "I." The basis of four heartbeats to one breath first appears during the course of the ninth and tenth years of life. It makes it possible for a child's soul to experience his or her own personality. The crisis that occurs around age nine or ten, the so-called "Rubicon," is merely the conscious awareness of the "I" which now comes in as a real, soul-experience.

Whereas in early childhood, breathing is more rapid and the blood has to pulse through the lungs at a ratio of more than four times per heartbeat (1:5 to 1:6), at around age nine, the healthy ratio of 1:4 can be achieved. However, this can happen only if the lungs branch out in the prescribed way and grow in length so that they can provide enough oxygen (and nitrogen).

Above and beyond this, the scope of the overlying rhythms is large. In the nervous system there are rhythms that are 0.001 to 0.1 seconds in length. The brain controls intensity of pain, sensations of warm and cold, impressions of color, sound perception, etc. by way of shorter or longer intervals between single nerve impulses (Rosslenbroich, 1994).

Within the rhythmic systems of blood circulation, respiration, peristalsis, etc. are found rhythms of between 150 waves per minute and one wave per hour. The lesser-known arterial basic vibration consists of about 150 waves per minute. Pulse fluctuates between 40 and 240 beats per minute and the number of breaths fluctuates accordingly between 10 and 60 per minute. Blood pressure fluctuates in a 10-second rhythm, and three rhythms of peristalsis overlap each other in the stomach. A peristaltic wave goes through the stomach about three times per minute, from top to bottom, to push the partially digested food into the duodenum. With every third wave, once per minute, there is a slightly stronger muscle contraction and once per hour there is a single, slow peristaltic wave in the stomach. There are about 12 peristaltic waves per minute in the small intestine (Rosslenbroich, 1994).

The waves in nighttime sleep phases (Schmidt and Thews, 1985) and the inclination to sleep during the day function in approximately a ninety-minute rhythm (ultradian rhythm; see Rosslenbroich, 1994). The cycle of waking and sleeping, the rhythms of metabolic activities in the liver and gallbladder, and many other bodily rhythms connected with pain sensitivity, composition of blood and urine, reaction capacity and so on follow a 24-hour rhythm (circadian rhythm; see Rosslenbroich, 1994).

In reference to the harmonious ratio of breath to pulse, it should be added that we are not talking about a rigid, inflexible breathing mechanism, but much more an average ratio of breathing to pulse during a resting state. In adults, during the day, this ratio fluctuates very strongly depending on mental and physical demands and is usually only at a 1:4 ratio during deep sleep. In addition, after age eleven children again experience a disturbance in the "healthy" breathing rhythm because of approaching puberty, during which part of the time there is a ratio of 1:3. Traces of immersion in earthly physicality are shown very clearly by the pulse frequency.

After external breathing, which has just been outlined, internal breathing begins inside the physical organism. Arterial blood transports inhaled gases — oxygen, nitrogen, carbon dioxide, and other very finely diluted gases — to the internal organs, the sense organs, muscles, and so on, where cellular respiration then takes place, whereby the cells receive essential substances and deposit waste into the venous bloodstream. As has already been mentioned, the flowing in and out and co-mingling of the life processes is also observable here. Cell metabolism, with its processes of nourishing, secreting, and maintaining, which are, in turn, the foundation for cellular growth and division (reproducing), cannot happen without the preceding breathing process, which provides oxygen to the cells, allows carbon dioxide to be carried away from the cells, and helps maintain a healthy body temperature (warming).

The internalization process of breathing in connection with the individuality can also be observed in the link between breathing and skeletal growth. Children re-form their own physical bodies from out of inherited structures. The form of the skeleton is primarily determined through movement, and movement, with regard to muscle tone is, again, affected by breathing. How a person creatively "sounds forth" with his or her body is directly connected to breathing. If a newborn is awake then the muscles are predominately in a hypertonic state, meaning tensed; but if asleep, the muscles are completely relaxed (hypotonic). This polar relationship changes the most intensively during the first year of life; so that, if someone is walking, about one-third of the muscles function to support the body's movement; a third of the muscles are relaxed; a third are in a middle state between tensed and relaxed and they, together with the relaxed muscles, are ready to engage in movement as needed. Just the changes that take place in the skeleton alone from newborn to adult demonstrate the effects of the breathing process.

In a newborn, formation of the sinus cavities (paranasal, frontal, maxillary) has not yet begun. They are formed through a process of pneumatization during the first seven years of life.

A newborn's spine, with its slightly sickle-shaped curvature, is not yet up to the task of standing upright. Children develop their capacity for motion at their own pace. At some point during this process, the supporting structure of the spine will be individually developed; always dependent upon muscle tone, which is affected by breathing. In the third year, approximately, the hips straighten out and the little tummy no longer pokes out into the world with each breath. Now the breathing undergoes some serious changes. The upper and lower parts of a human being are "separated" by the rhythmically moving diaphragm and "I"-consciousness awakens.

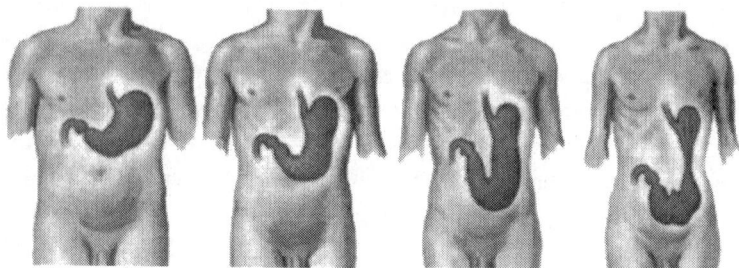

FIGURE 4
Different positions and forms of the stomach according to physique.
L to R: Hypertonic muscles, Orthotonic muscles, Hypotonic muscles, Atonic muscles.
Source: Netter, 2008

Through the internalization of breathing, the ribs, which were horizontally positioned in infancy, now turn downward toward the Earth's heaviness and form the structure of the chest cavity, which continues to grow within the established structure.

During the further course of development the limbs continue to transform and grow. This can be observed especially in the change from having slightly bowed legs to having slight knock-knees, and finally to the (hopefully) straight legs of the five-or-six-year-old child. With the re-shaping of the feet into a double arch, a person is lifted a step further away from the heaviness of Earth; ideally, the Achilles tendon is positioned at a right angle to the Earth.

One sees the breathing process in action in forms composed of flowing movement, but every soul disturbance — tension, stress, overwork, etc. — can cause an imbalance in this flow and change the healthy ratio.

Since many bodily organs mainly consist of muscle tissue, it is clear that the organ forms created in the first years of life are likewise influenced by the breathing process. Certainly, heredity plays a role in organ formation. The variable breathing process is also influenced by how the child is experiencing the surroundings, imitating adults, and becoming attuned to the soul-atmosphere of the environment; nevertheless, it is the breathing process that creates these forms, which are very particular in each individual. A person's individuality plays an important role in determining how to deal with the various influences. The established, individual structures remain with us during our further growth.

A Breathing Relationship with the World – Breathing of the Soul and Spirit

It can also be said that because human beings have a soul, they stand in continuous relationship with the environment. Physical exertion, the soul's expanding in joy or being burdened by sorrow, the kind of spirit activity that takes place during learning, studying, or reflection — all require intact breathing that is in harmony with the particular demands. For this reason, during hard physical labor or sports activities there is an impulse for rapid breathing with many pulse beats per breath so that the needed amount of oxygen is carried into the bloodstream. On the other hand, emotions such as happiness, fear, shock, or meditative immersion into the soul-spirit aspect, effect strong changes in breathing.

A breathing relationship with the world, which can be a physical expression of the soul-spirit through physical breathing, shows us to what a great extent the human being, as a whole, is a breathing being, and how breathing is very much a constantly changing process. The range of pulse beats per minute fluctuates between 40 in a resting state (often in puberty) and 240 at peak performance (in top-performing athletes). The ratio of pulse beats per breath ranges from 1:2.5 to 1:10.3 or more (Rosslenbroich, 1994).

As an aside, in connection with breathing of the soul and spirit, let us detour our thoughts to the subject of ongoing brain research; specifically, research on bonding behavior. We will leave this very broad subject to the reader because it would lead us too far off topic. However, it should be pointed out that there is clearly a close connection between the atmosphere within the bonding setting and the possibility of learning how to breathe in a healthy way, as well as the bonds created acting in our brain as the basis for cognitive functions (Gebauer and Hüther, 2004).

Incarnation of the Breathing Process

In child development, the breathing process has to slowly find its way into physicality. As mentioned previously, infants inhale and exhale relatively small amounts of air, breathing and pulse are more rapid, and the ratio of breath to pulse is higher. During waking states breathing is relatively susceptible to sensory impressions and emotional stress. Therefore, there is a greater exchange of oxygen and heat through the skin; which is why, where infants are concerned, one speaks of a breathing relationship to the world that is not yet so deeply penetrated into physicality, but much more on the periphery. The physical expression of this is that infant lungs are only incompletely formed (see Figures 1 and 2) and they have comparably thin, translucent skin.

There is something else in infants that is not really physically driven, and that is the area of the bodily rhythms. A human being is not only a breathing being in connection with the lungs (physical), soul impulses (astral), and spirit activities ("I"), but also in the area of living functions (etheric). Understood as a process, breathing does not only take hold in the lungs and blood circulation that is dependent upon them, but also moves into all of the life processes as rhythm. In a certain respect the stomach and intestines also breathe, but it is not breathing in the normal sense; rather, it is the life process of breathing, which is expressed as peristalsis in that area of the body.

It is likewise so with the sleeping-waking rhythm and the many other rhythms dependent upon it; for instance, sensitivity to pain and cold, composition of the blood and urine, and all the other rhythmically oriented organ functions (Rosslenbroich, 1994). They are all breathing processes because there is a breathing-like exchange between activity and rest, tension and relaxation.

Physical rhythms are not yet fully perfected in children. They must first be learned, or, to say it more precisely, the preconditions which allow the life process of breathing to integrate into physicality have to slowly mature and ripen.

That is to say, after birth an infant is still very non-rhythmic. She does not recognize day or night, and the good intentions of parents regarding regular feeding times are met by a baby who completely lacks a rhythmic sense. A baby has to gradually learn about, and cooperate with, the division of day and night, as well as regular feeding times.

Lack of a rhythmic sense also shows itself in infants' digestive processes. Sometimes they have a full diaper twice a day and sometimes it is five times a day. Consistent urine and stool elimination normalizes during the course of the toddler years. That means, however, that the bodily rhythms, understood to be breathing processes, only gradually gain control of the internal organs and their functions.

From this perspective, they are cosmic rhythms which, during the course of childhood, are introduced into the physical body in such a way that they become bodily rhythms. Initially, the body itself follows a genetically determined 25-hour rhythm. If one examines sleeping curve charts of infants whose sleeping times are not subjected to outside influences, there is a daily shifting of sleep times by about one hour (Rosslenbroich, 1994). Even adults, when put into an isolation chamber for a period of time without any external indicators of light and darkness or an alarm clock, revert back to a genetically predetermined 25-hour rhythm (Schmidt and Lang, 2007).

The 25-hour sleeping-waking rhythm also puts all the other daily-rhythm fluctuations of organ functions (see above), such as the digestive organs, liver, gallbladder, and so forth, onto a 25-hour rhythm. Replacing the inherited Moon rhythm with a 24-hour Sun rhythm is a cultural-educational task which adults themselves must constantly work on in order to maintain a healthy relationship to day and night, and to the environment. It is the sun rhythm that first brings healthy rhythms inside the physical body. That is why Waldorf education places such a high value on a sensible and rhythmically integrated daily routine in the home, kindergarten and school. This knowledge is supported by more and more studies coming out about the ill effects of nighttime and shift work (Ackerman, 2008).

The tasks for education resulting from this knowledge are addressed in the chapter "The Seven Life Processes in Education."

Breathing as a Condition for Incarnation

Rudolf Steiner presented these ideas about learning "correct" breathing and sleeping at the beginning of his lecture series *Study of Man* (GA 293) in Stuttgart in 1919:

> *Of all the relationships a human being has with the external world, the most important among them is breathing. ... If we look at a child, in referring to his or her being, we have to say: 'This child has not yet learned to breathe in such a way that breathing supports the nerve-sense process in the right way.' ... But there is something else a child cannot yet do correctly and this other thing has to be gotten under control so that harmony is produced between the two members of being; the physical body and the soul-spirit. What a child cannot do correctly at the beginning of his existence (you will have noticed that usually things which we must highlight as spiritual seem to contradict the order of things in the external world), is make the switch between sleeping and waking in a way that is appropriate to being human. ... Internally, that which lies at the foundation of sleeping and waking; a child cannot yet undertake that.*

After birth, human babies sleep sixteen hours or more per day. However, sleep research confirms that the portion of that time spent in REM sleep (REM = Rapid Eye Movement), with tensed muscles, rapid eye movement and a stronger tendency to dream, is about 50% in infants and sinks to about 20% over the course of childhood into adulthood (see Figure 5).

The core message in the first lecture of the *Study of Man* series (GA 293) is that the soul-spirit aspects of a human being only gradually connect with the physical aspect. This has become a practical task of Waldorf education: to make it possible for breathing and sleeping to occur in the right way so that the connection between soul-spirit bodies and the physical body can be solidly successful.

If the switch between waking and sleeping is understood as an expression of the breathing process, which only gradually finds its way into the physical body, then, from the viewpoint of the seven life processes, we have gained a deeper understanding of the subject of learning to breathe and to sleep, as it is presented in the first lecture in the *Study of Man* series.

If we once again bring up the idea that it is the etheric element that connects the physical body and the soul-spirit aspects, then it becomes clear that there has to be a correlation between integration of a life process into the physical body and the soul faculties that emerge from it. The breathing process should form the basis for our further understanding of these concepts.

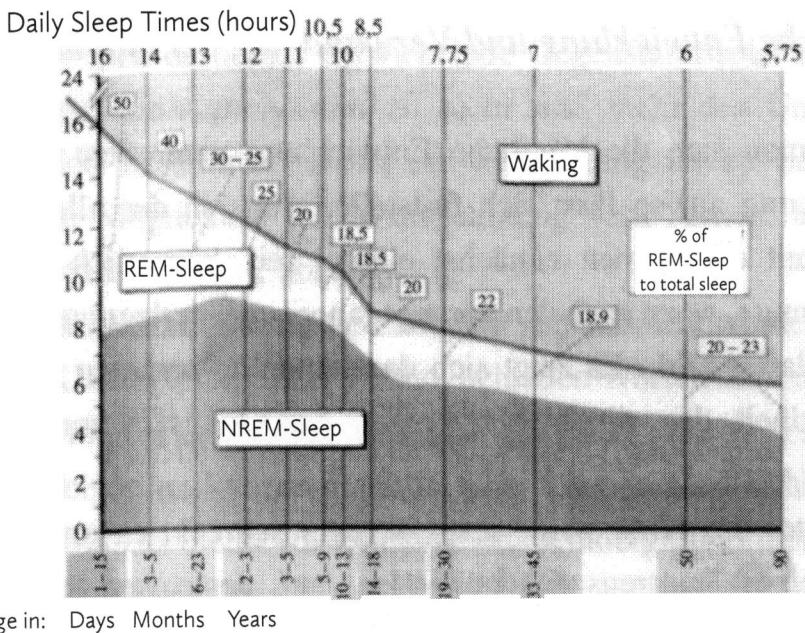

Daily Sleep Times (hours) 10,5 8,5

16 14 13 12 11 10 7,75 7 6 5,75

Waking

REM-Sleep

% of
REM-Sleep
to total sleep

NREM-Sleep

Age in: Days Months Years

FIGURE 5
Ratio of REM to Non-REM phases during sleep.
Source: Schmidt and Lang, 2007

Child Development and the Transformation of Breathing

Looking at childhood development from the aspect of breathing, it can be determined that in the very first moments of life, purely from a physical viewpoint, breathing has to be learned. In light of the aforementioned considerations, sleeping would have to included in that process as well. During the course of childhood it becomes apparent that the breathing process very gradually becomes more and more autonomous.

The older an infant is, the less often she will be startled out of sleep by a creaking floorboard, or become breathless with the least bit of tension in the surroundings, and the more she will be able to rise above physicality and draw on those first, very dulled sense experiences in the first few weeks of life, experiences which are not accessible to consciousness. The first sensory experience is fixing the gaze on an object, followed by control over the neck muscles and lifting the head, "conscious" grasping, turning, belly crawling, hands and knees crawling, sitting, and, finally, standing upright.

During this time, through gradually becoming accustomed to the physical body, the motion patterns of early childhood are vanquished; which is directly connected to breathing. All of this will only work if breathing is stable enough so that energy is left over for one's own sense perceptions.

The interaction between *sense perception*, primarily at first through the lower senses (touch, life-sense, balance and the sense of one's own movements) and breathing is easily recognized in body-play during the first few months of life. (See Lindenberg 2004, and Soesman 2001). Every child finds his own tempo in movement and "listening to" movement. The increasing development of a balance between muscle tension and release of muscle tension during movement is exactly the area where the effects of the breathing process are most visible; play with objects, which develops out of this balance, shows the child's ability to turn his *attention* to the surroundings more and more. It should be kept in mind that, from the beginning, the possibility of sense perception is dependent upon breathing, even from a neurological standpoint.

Later, the ability to devote attention to something becomes more developed, which allows kindergartners to follow what adults are saying, be occupied with an object for more than one or two minutes, and even quietly listen to a short story. In interacting with kindergartners one quickly notices that the children whose breathing is harmonious, even, and quiet are accepting of the daily rhythm; they are easily at play and are able to stop playing when it is time to eat, sing, or listen to a story. Children who give one an impression of breathlessness are quickly unsettled by any movement in the room and are either compelled to move or make comments about it when anything happens in their surroundings; these children's souls are not yet able to "breathe in and out" in the correct way where the happenings in their surroundings are concerned. They are still too strongly occupied with just letting breathing and other physical rhythmic processes happen, and do not yet have much energy left over for giving their full attention to something.

Integration of the breathing process causes the release of certain soul faculties; thus one of the seven life processes, the breathing process, shows the connection between etheric forces and the human capacity for thought, imagination, and memory.

The aspects we have just described — the slow transformation of breathing, the integration of physical rhythms into the internal organs through breathing, waking, and sleeping, as well as the unfolding of soul faculties through the gradual anchoring of the breathing process — bring us to the question of the deeper meaning of this process of development, which is extremely long compared to that of animals. The first consideration in searching for this meaning is surely the necessity of understanding the living processes for human beings to act not only in a way that is bound by instinct, but rather, after a long period of development up to the age of majority, to mature into freedom. This is the result of the presence of the "I" in human beings. The necessity of the "I" grappling with all these living processes does not exist in animals.

Additionally, a second consideration is the need for the first three years of childhood to be free from demands on the faculties of attention and concentration. The unfolding of the basic human faculties of standing and walking upright, speaking, and thinking requires something besides walking, speaking, and thinking role models on the Earth; it also requires being bound together with, and under the protection of, higher beings. The first three years are primarily characterized by a child developing these three exclusively human faculties without an awake consciousness and therefore without an "I"-consciousness. Uprightness, speech, and thought are, in a manner of speaking, given as gifts by the three lowest angelic hierarchies. (We are not referring to abstract thinking here, but rather the ability to make correlations between various things in the surroundings: "Baker bakes bread – Mommy bakes bread – Mommy is a baker!") In a lecture given on April 28, 1923 (GA 224), Rudolf Steiner explained that the ability to stand upright and walk was the result of the influence of the Archai, the ability to speak and become familiar with the mother tongue is the work of the archangels (Archangeloi), and the ability to think is the result of the influence of the angels (Angeloi).

However, these "gifts from Heaven" need the protection of those who have a wakened consciousness directed toward the Earth and who turn their concentrated attention to earthly requirements. These are the years in which the efficacy of the Christ-principle for development can unfold (Steiner, *The Spiritual Guidance of the Individual and Humanity*, GA 15).

Realization of the words, "I am the way, the truth, and the life" (walking – speaking – thinking), is achieved with the help of the angelic hierarchies named above. Where wakened consciousness is in control, things are grasped and taken in hand; where dreamy consciousness is in control, no amount of directing attention toward earthly requirements will stand in the way of a connection with higher beings. In adulthood, certainly, one can seek out a connection with Christ; in very young children the connection already exists, just without an awakened "I"-consciousness. From this perspective, it is not only simply a law of nature which dictates that soul faculties only very slowly unfold from out of the integration of the breathing process, and all the other life processes as well; at the same time, there is a great amount of wise and indispensable protection involved so that a child's soul does not have at its disposal the same soul faculties which will be needed later to deal with earthly requirements. Protection of the soul, which prevents it from being mainly occupied with earthly conditions — something that is called forth from out of the "I"-consciousness — promotes the possibility of a child being guided by the angelic hierarchies during the decisively important first three years of life. Recognition of the deeper meaning in human development is made possible through this.

Warming

Warming, or warmth production, is the second life process. It is made possible by the breathing process.

In the mother's womb an independent warming process was not yet necessary. The constant warmth of the womb created ideal conditions for the baby to thrive. With birth came the necessity to hold one's own against fluctuating temperatures and enter into a healthy relationship with the outside world through an independent life process. The warmth sense, the perception of warmth, is not what is meant here, but rather the creation of one's own, inner warmth in a healthy relationship to the external world.

Initially, in contrast to breathing, the warmth life process is not so reliably activated in tiny bodies. Even though the breathing process is also very susceptible to influences and often inconsistent, a child always breathes, as long as there is no pathologic dysfunction present in the lungs — in heat, in cold, whether awake or sleeping, healthy or ill, there are no exceptions. On the other hand, warmth is dependent upon external care in the form of warm, protective clothing. (The fact that breathing also requires external care has already been indicated, and will be clarified in the chapter titled "The Seven Life Processes in Education.")

The warming process, or rather, healthy adaptation to the environment, moves further and further into physicality just as the breathing process does. As a child gets older, this leads to achieving a certain amount of independence from the temperature in the surroundings. As adults we can go for longer periods of time being too lightly dressed without the threat of becoming immediately ill. Blood circulation to the body's periphery and the development of warmth through metabolic and muscle activity proceed unimpaired and in such a sophisticated way that one can see just how autonomous the internal life of the body has become in regard to external temperatures. From a physical standpoint, this has to do with a well-functioning blood circulation system, as well as with the skin, which, during the course of childhood has become a well-defined protective sheath. From a non-physical standpoint, one could say that through breathing the soul-spirit aspect gains an interface with the warmth-ether forces, and that the warmth process is activated by connection with the physical body.

In anthroposophical spiritual science, warmth is not described as a measurable condition of matter, but rather as a sophisticated, disseminating, infinitely subtle element that originates in cosmic worlds. Breathing creates a connection to the etheric forces of the macro-cosmos and the act of inhaling air allows a human being to begin to create his or her own formative-forces body. Warmth in the physical body, even into the furthest branches of the bloodstream, is made possible by a connection with the world-warmth-ethers (Steiner, *Illness and Therapy*, GA 313).

With this life process, from a phenomenological standpoint, one can clearly observe how the relationship a human being has with the world of the surroundings changes during childhood. Infants are still so highly impressionable that they are not in a position to insulate themselves from environmental temperatures; without warm clothing they would suffer a

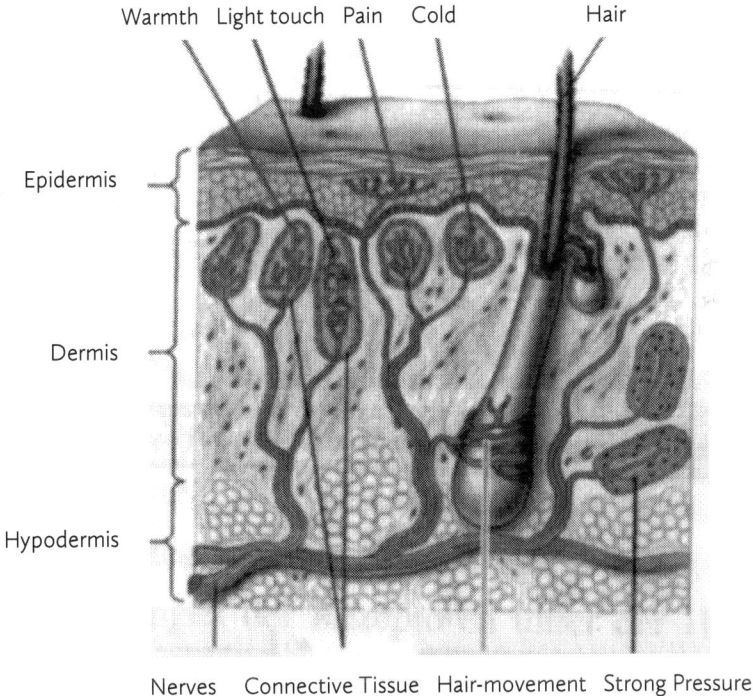

FIGURE 6

Various sensory receptors under the skin.
Source: Campbell and Reece, 1997

tremendous loss of body heat. Immediately after birth, even with an external temperature of 37°C (98.6°F), a naked infant would still suffer from hypothermia; loss of heat through a newborn's thin skin is so great that one cannot dispense with warmed blankets followed by warm clothing and a hat, even in the heat of summer. Even a six-month-old baby being outside in temperatures under 0°C (32°F), wearing a hat, scarf and mittens, will often exhibit signs of frostbite on the cheeks if a protective ointment has not been applied beforehand.

Six, seven, or eight years later, body warmth production is already developed to the point that its relationship to outside temperatures is significantly different. A child of early school-age is usually able to run through the snow barefoot without any problem. Just a few minutes later the child returns to a warm house with increased blood circulation in feet that were exposed to the cold; children now seem to warm up again "on their own." It is a kind of bodily self-awareness that gradually increases into adulthood.

The warming process is observed not only as it relates to a whole human being within the environment, but also as a process differentiated within the body; and is therefore a highly health-promoting process.

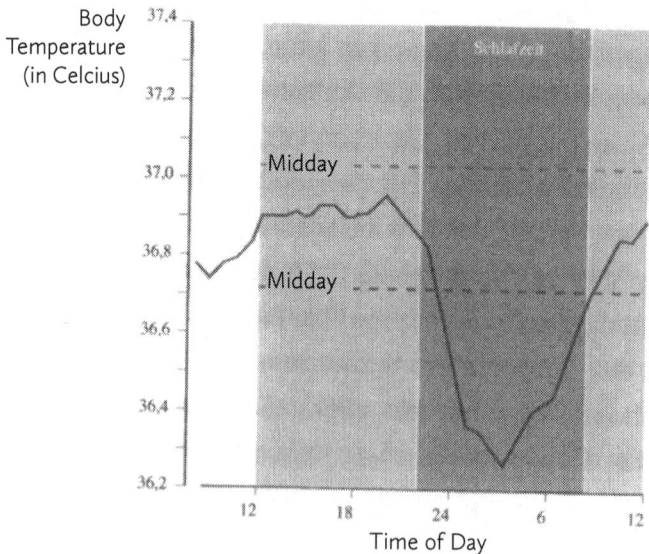

FIGURE 7

Daily core body temperature.
Source: Schmidt and Lang, 2007

The so-called body core temperature is approximately 37°C (98.6°F); in contrast, the liver measures approximately 41°C (105.8°F), the heart 38 to 39°C (100.4 to 102.2°F) and the lungs 35 to 36°C (95 to 96.8°F) (Husemann and Wolf, 2003).

Upon closer examination, the connection with the breathing processes becomes immediately clear because the body core temperature fluctuates during the course of the day. 37°C (98.6°F) is just an approximation of day-time body temperature. Actually, the human warmth production system "breathes," often resulting in an early morning rectal temperature measuring under 36.5°C (97.7°F) and in the early evening approximately 37°C (98.6°F). (See Figure 7.) It can be observed that when we are awake we are warmer internally (core warmth), but while sleeping the warmth spreads to the periphery of the body (warmth mantle).

During the waking state the skin usually has a temperature of over 30°C (86°F), with the exception of cold feet. A healthy target temperature lies between 33 and 35°C (91.4 and 95°F). Then the sensory stimuli for the heat and cold receptors under the skin are in a balanced state (area of in-difference); no sensation of temperature takes place, but rather a state of comfort.

Additionally, heat and cold receptors under the skin play an important role in body temperature regulation. Sensations of warmth and cold are transported to the brain via nerve pathways (the physiological basis for the sense of warmth). But that is not the only thing; the *difference* between skin and core temperature as well as an *increase* or *decrease* in the same is also recognized — a very dynamic process!

The sensory perceptions of the receptors under the skin, as well as the so-called thermoreceptors inside the body, flow together in the hypothal-amus, a small part of the brain located close to the optic chiasm, where the two optic nerves cross over each other. Here temperature differenc-es, increases and decreases, lead to corresponding *reactions.* This not only describes the physiological basis of the sense of warmth, but also of the *warmth production* that is of interest to us here.

One can distinguish four kinds of temperature regulation controlled mainly by the hypothalamus, two of which take place under the skin.

Dilation and constriction of the capillaries directly under the skin: When external temperature increases, these tiny blood vessels under the skin di-late for better circulation, or rather, a larger blood surface area. Because of this, the skin, which has become warmer on the inside, releases more heat into the external environment. On the other hand, when external tempera-ture falls, the arteries under the skin constrict. Then skin temperature de-creases; however, internal body temperature can be more easily maintained

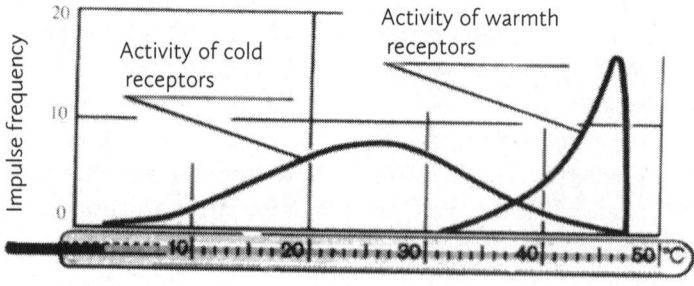

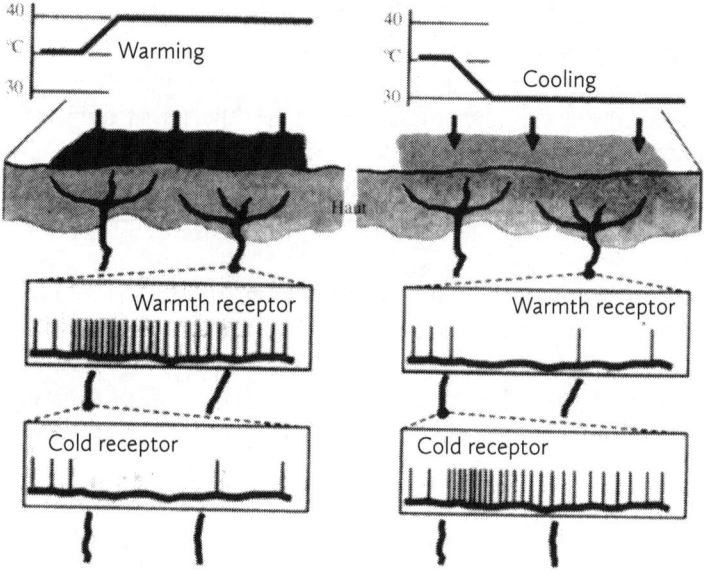

FIGURE 8

Diagram of the impulse frequency of warmth and cold receptors; above and below is where the activity of these receptors takes place.

Source: Klinke and Silbernagel, 1996

at a constant level because warm blood has less contact with external cold.

Perspiration: When the body is threatened with overheating, sweat glands under the skin are activated. The resulting evaporative cooling causes the skin's surface to be cooler in spite of dilated blood vessels, which can then contribute to cooling of the blood. Even so, during athletic activities the body core temperature rises to 38 to 39°C (100.4 to 102.2°F), which, by the way, leads to still higher performance levels.

Changes in breathing frequency: The more rapid breathing is, the more blood pulses along the large surface area of the lungs, which will cause it to cool down a bit, just as happens with dilated blood vessels under the skin. On the other hand, with slower breathing and pulse the blood comes into less contact with the cooler external environment of the skin and lungs, so that a constant internal temperature can be maintained.

Warmth production in the metabolic-limb system: The act of transforming the energy contained in food into new substance combinations releases heat. Internal organs are especially involved in this. However, metabolic processes also take place in every single cell, which contribute to the development of warmth. Additionally, heat is produced wherever there is muscle activity. For this reason, in the language of science, one speaks of burning consumed substances during metabolic and muscle activity. Therefore, food also contains a certain calorific value expressed in terms of kJ (kilojoules) and kcal (kilocalories). One can even convert the calculation to measure physical output such as watts or horsepower, but that is not useful for our purpose here.

This is natural science's legitimate explanation of the warming process, but it can be expanded if one includes certain aspects of anthroposophical knowledge. Following on the four points described above, one could also say: Because humans stand in the world as breathing beings, the warmth process is able to be incorporated into the physical body in a healthy way, or rather, the connection to the "warmth principle" can be found. Connected to this is the question of how other people look at and treat a person, and of whether one was able to grow up in an atmosphere of warmth and protection. It is not possible to consider each life process as something independent. This is made especially apparent in the body's production of sweat, which involves the secreting process as well.

Consider the fact that the human organism can take energy in the form of sugar or starch from grains, vegetables, or fruits that have ripened in the sun, release it, and, by the circuitous route of nutrition deep in its internal regions, deal with sun-energy and freely control this energy — this is already one aspect of the nourishing process.

All metabolic and muscle activity, no matter how small, has to do with an inversion of the effects of the sun: actual warmth development from out of food substances. What I do with this released warmth, how I implement it, whether for thinking or hard, physical work, remains my free choice as a human being. An animal's use of this energy is bound by instinct and used for its existence as an animal being. Through the ego ("I"), a human being has the possibility of illuminating his actions with intention. (See Steiner, *The Riddle of Humanity*, lecture 7, GA 170.)

We have now come closer to an understanding of the physiological basis for the body's ability to heat and cool itself. Increased or decreased metabolic activity, changing breathing frequency, perspiration, and dilation or constriction of blood vessels under the skin, are all made use of by the sensory receptors for heat and cold (among other things) in order to activate the appropriate processes of temperature regulation at the right time.

Soul and Spirit Warming

The human organism does not react to temperatures in the surroundings solely through regulation of the described processes; it is influenced by soul and spirit to a high degree. For instance, from the viewpoint of the soul, the emotion of happiness precipitates a different body temperature than that of fear. A happy person is able to devote herself to the outside world with more confidence and sympathy, which leads to stronger blood circulation and a different form of air exhalation — through laughter, for instance. On the other hand, fear or shock causes the blood vessels under the skin to constrict, producing paleness and, in extreme cases, shivering. (Shivering begins when the usual forms of temperature regulation are not enough to maintain constant body temperature and the shivering motion then creates the needed warmth.)

From the viewpoint of the spirit, intellectual activity, loving thoughts, or enthusiasm for a certain ideal — a kind of infusion of soul into mental activities — affect soul perceptions in such a way that they in turn penetrate into the physical body and its warming process. The opposite occurs with mental apathy or a "cold" intellect, which disengages thoughts from the emotional stimuli of sympathy and antipathy.

One could also name free-wheeling thought as among the things that are disengaged from the emotions that affect the physical body's tendencies for warming and cooling. If thinking, feeling, and willing are not intertwined with each other to a healthy degree, thoughts without enthusiasm will occur, so that they will have no effect on the human warmth process. It is a life of imagination without any enthusiasm or radiance, and also no consequences in the life of the will.

Since a human being is, first and foremost, a spirit-being whose individuality is bound together in a structured arrangement of soul (astral body), life (etheric) body, and physical body, from an anthroposophical viewpoint the warmth processes depend on the impulses of the soul and spirit. These warmth processes, called forth from out of soul-spirit warmth, must first take hold of the etheric-life processes over the course of childhood. However, in order to accomplish this they need certain inherited physical traits which make possible the integration of the warming process by providing healthy nerve pathways, a functional brain, a heart, unhindered blood circulation, functional metabolic organs, and so on.

Integration of the Warming Process in Child Development and Its Transformation

After birth, upon emerging from the amniotic fluid sac with its temperature of 37°C (98.6°F), a newborn is immediately confronted with the element of air. Besides the breathing process that now begins, the body also has to deal with external temperature. Conditions under the skin, with its watery elements of tissue, blood, and so forth, are so different from conditions of the air that this initially presents too much of a challenge. An infant's enormous loss of heat — even with an external temperature of 37°C (98.6°F) — is caused by its inability to adequately regulate blood vessel dilation and constriction, breathing frequency, perspiration, and metabolic activity as they relate to maintaining a constant body core temperature. It is imperative to counteract this inability to self-regulate internal temperature by providing warm clothing, including a hat. On the other hand, an infant's body can do nothing to prevent overheating because of too much clothing that does not "breathe," heat accumulation, or being under a heavy down blanket, to name a few examples. The warming process is still so imperfectly anchored in physicality that this task must be assumed by the child's parents and caregivers. It is their responsibility to ensure the child has clothing and bedding that "breathes" (real wool is the best), and always ensure that the right amount of heat is present. The process of healthy adjustment to the environment, with adequate warmth production (but not too much) is facilitated from the outside through soul-spirit warmth in the surroundings, which is created through adults' real, loving interest in the child.

With time, it can be observed how a child begins with self-guided, warmth-producing activities. Although a two-year-old will quickly become chilled sitting quietly in a wet sandbox, the active phases during which physical warmth is created increase more and more from the beginning of the crawling stage, and even more when a child learns to walk, run and jump. During the course of the second year of life, a child's occasional sweating tends to be more for the purpose of helping with a healthy cool-down, something that had to be supported through adult care in the first few months of life, because sweating in a baby could lead to far too much release of body heat.

One can observe the connection between the physical possibility of a healthy warmth-relationship with the environment and the interesting activities of crawling, walking and forming syllables and words. *Interest* in the world is connected with the physical capacity for heating and cooling. Later, in kindergarten, the connection becomes even more apparent. A child with warm hands and a healthy sense of whether or not it is necessary to take off a sweater is usually interested in play. It may not be lively games with other children, necessarily; it could be taking an interest in physical laws like gravity while building a wooden-block tower or dumping out a basket of chestnuts.

In contrast, a child with a delicate constitution, who is pale, with a tendency to having cold hands, may find it more difficult to find her own interests. Such children usually need a longer "lead-in time" during which they can observe before deciding to play with a toy or become involved in play situations.

The connection between warmth and children's interest is even more apparent if one once observes a real "hot-head." The child runs around in a T-shirt, red-faced and often sweating, while all the other children are wearing sweaters. Even so, this child still feels he is too warm. At home, with friends, relatives, or in the kindergarten, he impulsively gets right into some kind of play activity. Oftentimes, even the most understanding adults will have to put the brakes on with these children because otherwise something could get damaged, or there is concern for the safety of others. The child's interest goes overboard, in a manner of speaking, and sparks (or ignites) impulsive actions. This phenomenon can be observed in adults too in the intensity and impulsiveness of some of their spontaneous behavior, or if someone is yelling and in a real rage. In this case, enthusiasm and interest, just as in the physical system of warmth production, are less restrained. There is no longer an established relationship between the external and internal worlds, but rather the external world is being heated from the inside; that goes for physical as well as mental and emotional warmth. This brings about the danger of a lack of "I"-presence inside the physical body. Heat is constantly diverted to the outside, which can lead to a lack of self-awareness. To meet such children with an attitude of gentleness and caution is a challenging responsibility for the educator.

A further step in the successive transformation of warmth production in connection with breathing is represented by the ability to *concentrate*. It is a step toward true attentiveness when a child is able not only to pay attention, listen, and quietly eat at the table, but also is able to really concentrate on something of interest or something in the environment which he wishes to imitate. This ability intensifies during the sixth year and is an indicator of school-readiness. From the way in which children can concentrate out of their own initiative, without pressure, it can be determined to what extent warmth-production and breathing have withdrawn from their exclusive task of physical body formation and are now able to bring the faculties of perception, attentiveness, and concentration to school subjects. As an adult, you can easily observe in yourself the connection between breathing, warmth production, and concentration. Just take note of your own ability to concentrate if you have gotten a shock, for example, or are excited about something, and your breathing is rapid and shallow, or if you are breathing heavily due to physical activity. You will notice that you first have to take a deep breath before you can concentrate.

In the first seven-year stage of life, the warming life process, interacting with breathing, develops the soul faculty of concentration. This faculty always suffers if the etheric element has to turn more of its energy back to the physical body so that adequate physical regeneration is possible in instances of exhaustion, nervousness, illness, or just fatigue.

A further step in child development can be observed when a child's interest is occupied with more than just his own movements, speech, thoughts, and the processes of physical formation. That is when real *enthusiasm* develops for something very specific, such as a certain kind of play stimulated by the imagination. In spite of this, interest in play and activities varies widely from day to day and minute to minute in three-, four- and five-year-olds. Only during the course of the sixth year, and more so in the seventh year, do interests arise that survive more than a single day. It could be specific games, a certain toy, a lasting delight in some household tasks or handwork, increased interest in painting or making music, and so on.

Three- or four-year-old children like to help set the table because they are simply imitating what they see and immerse themselves into the adult's stream of activity. In contrast, a six-year-old may become so interested and enthusiastic about the aesthetics of table-setting that she decides on the spur of the moment to set the table every morning from now on; and she will hold to that decision for some time. The child is now in a position to be able to *concentrate* for longer periods of time.

Added to that is the ability to *adapt* behavior to a specific situation so that it is appropriate for outer circumstances. For example, three-year-olds cannot make a reasonable choice of clothing based on the outside temperature. They depend upon adults to make that decision. Such a decision is much easier for a seven-year-old.

It is the same with assessing a specific social situation. If a child is already able to regulate body temperature in a healthy way, according to corresponding conditions, he is usually able to notice that many of the other children want to listen when the kindergarten teacher tells a story. Very young children are not yet able to do that. They cheerfully chatter about whatever comes to mind during the story.

The way and extent to which *interest, concentration, enthusiasm,* and *adaptability* are able to develop help determine to what extent the warming life process is already autonomously presiding over the physical body. This also involves the extent to which the forces produced by the warming process during early childhood, used to adapt to external temperatures in a healthy way and make possible temperature regulation of the individual internal organs, have been released, allowing for real, soul-spirit interest in the world. This is a basic precondition for school, because otherwise there is no interest in school subjects such as the alphabet, counting, or music. Learning from current life circumstances (implicit learning) is replaced by a type of learning that is explained, understood and remembered (explicit learning).

Thus we may describe how the warming process, anchored in the physical body, is connected with the soul faculties that grow out of it.

In conclusion, we may say about the interweaving effects of the life processes: Breathing gives the impulse for warmth production by stimulating blood circulation. The heart beats as a result of the movement of blood. (Embryology informs us that the blood does not circulate because the heart "pumps"; rather, the heart begins to beat because the blood moves!) Blood is now channeled to the skin, liver, sensory organs, etc., which leads to the warming of those areas. Metabolic activity in the liver, for instance, with its processes of nourishing, secreting, and maintaining, releases heat into the venous bloodstream which then leads to the heart, which can, in turn, result in changes in breathing because of the body's unconscious, internal awareness. A human being continuously lives within a dulled perception of the life processes, which always "run over and above and in and out of each other," but normally lie below the threshold of waking consciousness and only allow themselves to be precisely separated by way of intellectual reasoning. *In reality,* all seven life processes, intertwined and interconnected, occur in the entire physical organism with every single breath.

Nourishing

The third life process is nourishing, by which we mean not only the physical intake of nourishment, but also taking in sensory impressions, emotions and moods, and intellectual subject matter. There are soul-spirit aspects to be observed alongside physical, functional phenomena, as in the processes of breathing and warming.

Normally, the word "nourishing" is referring to the act of physically taking in and processing food substances. "I nourish myself with something" means: I take in, break down, release substances, and then integrate these substances, in partially new combinations, back into my physical organism. That is actually a description of the metabolic process. From an anthroposophical viewpoint, the definitions of nourishment and metabolism can be broadened in regard to the release of etheric formative forces bound up with nutrition, which maintain the physical body not only in the material sense, but also in the living-functional sense. They protect it from degeneration, decay, and failure of living forms and functions.

> Now, it is certainly important that a person eat every day. However, most of what is eaten daily is absolutely not there to be taken into the body as matter and then deposited. The major portion is there for the purpose of giving the forces it contains to the body, which will stimulate it to activity. Most of what is taken into the body in this way is eliminated again; so that one must say that metabolism is not a system of weights and measures, but rather, metabolism is concerned with the question of whether, by eating food, we are able to correctly receive into ourselves the living quality of the forces it contains; because we need this living quality when we walk, for instance, or work, or even when we move our arms" (Steiner, The Agriculture Course, lecture 4, GA 327).

Anthroposophical knowledge of nature and human beings informs us that whole-grain products from biodynamic agriculture feed human beings in a living way. The etheric structure of root vegetables supports the nerve-sense system in the human organism, leaf and stem vegetables the rhythmic system, and flowers and fruits support and strengthen metabolism and the limb-system (See Steiner, From Sunspots to Strawberries, lecture 6, GA 354).

This is one of the aspects of knowledge defined within the concept of nourishment that includes at least three of the seven life processes. Taking in and disintegrating matter or a living structure is possible through the life process of *nourishing*. Sorting of broken-apart substances and etheric forces is made possible by the life process of *secreting*: Substances are sorted according to whether they will remain on the inside (utilization) or go to the outside (secretion, elimination). Substances are broken apart, either mechanically, through chewing, or chemically by saliva and gastric acid, among other things. Preserving the health of decaying structures and processes in the physical body, as well as successful transportation of utilized substances is made possible by the life process of *maintaining*. Since *growing* and *reproducing* are possible only if there is a functioning metabolic system, the result is that there are five life processes dependent upon what is commonly referred to as nourishing.

But here we will be dealing exclusively with the *life process* of nourishing. Since it is closely connected with the secreting life process, concentrating solely on the nourishing process presents a challenge to our thinking. Nevertheless, it is necessary to undertake the challenge if one wishes to focus on the differentiation of life into seven separate processes.

Food Intake

With physical nutritional processes, nourishment and secretion are interconnected. The nourishing process is never solely a process of ingestion. Already in the mouth an isolated substance has to be dealt with; namely saliva, which, activated by the sense of smell, makes an important contribution to the dissolution of food through its enzymes and consistency, along with the chewing action of the teeth.

Digestion intermingles the processes of nourishing and secreting, but it is still possible to identify a functional difference between the two. The nourishing process involves everything that is taken in and merged together. The secreting process involves everything to do with ordering and sorting for utilization inside the body, or for elimination and secretion outside the body. During the breakdown of food substances these two processes meet.

Production of saliva and gastric acid is already influenced during food preparation by smells and visual presentation, without which no dissolution and disintegration would be possible. That is to say, secretions are induced which make possible the subsequent nourishment process. The next step is merging the various foodstuffs in the mouth. Through chewing actions the lips, tongue, and teeth mechanically masticate, while the enzymes of the secreted saliva perform the initial chemical breakdown of the food. Besides this pre-digestive activity, softening of the food by the warm, liquid saliva is what allows tasting and swallowing of the masticated food (bolus) in the first place.

Through rhythmic contractions of the esophagus, the masticated food next lands in the stomach and comes into contact with secreted gastric acid (diluted hydrochloric acid). In the stomach the bolus is thoroughly mixed and moved in the direction of the duodenum by regular contractions of the stomach muscles, which take place about every 20 seconds. Also in the stomach, carbohydrates, proteins and fat are separated by gastric acids and their structures have begun to be broken down. Once again, we see how the two processes, nourishment and secretion, meet together.

The bolus remains in the stomach from one to seven hours (Renz-Polster and Krautzig, 2008) depending on the amount of complex proteins and fats that have to be tackled by the gastric acids, and is pushed in small portions into the duodenum.

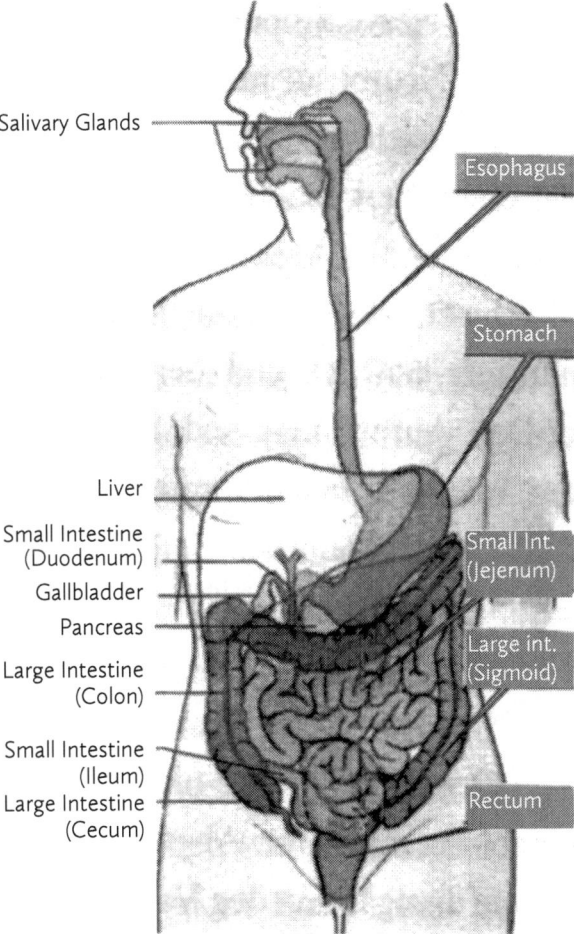

FIGURE 9

Positions of the digestive organs in the abdominal cavity.

Source: Klinke and Silbernagel, 1996

There is now contact with the enzyme-rich secretions of the pancreas. The first thing they do is to neutralize the gastric acids, and the second is to continue to break down the carbohydrates, proteins, and fats.

One can clearly see that within the life process of nourishing, its processes of food intake, merging together, and separating are always tied in with secretions, without which the nourishment process could not take place. In the mouth is saliva, in the stomach is gastric acid, and in the pancreas are neutralizing secretions.

This is similar to the processing of sensory impressions. Taking in and processing an impression of pain, cold, color, or sound can only happen successfully with the help of secreted substances. A sense impression creates a nerve impulse, which is carried via a neurotransmitter, a chemical substance that is released at the end of a nerve fiber and, by diffusing across the synapse or junction, causes the transfer of the impulse to another nerve fiber (Reichert, 2000). See also the section on "Secreting."

It is difficult to clearly formulate where the life process of nourishing ends and that of secreting begins. Taking in and merging together food, sensory impressions, and intellectual subject matter always requires the involvement of the secreting life process; that is to say, in the physical realm it needs certain secretions, and in the soul-spirit realm it requires analytic activity (see the section "Integration of the Secreting Life Process during the First Seven Years and Its Transformation").

There are further complex connections between individual internal organs, especially the gallbladder with its release of bile produced in the liver into the digestive tract, but we will not go into detail about these here. There is also the liver with its "conditioning" and cleaning of the blood and the production (*reproduction*) of the most varying types of cells. These are all special contributions to the success of the nourishing process, including nutrition for the cells, sensory organs, and many other things.

Nourishing the Soul and Spirit

The physical body is not the only thing that needs nourishment or food which, with the help of the life processes of nourishing, secreting, and maintaining, is taken in, broken down and reorganized; the human soul needs nourishment too. As mentioned in previous chapters, the preconditions for perceiving impressions are, first of all, a breathing relationship with the world and, secondly, warmth and harmony of soul, out of which come interest, enthusiasm, and concentration. If these preconditions are present, then impressions can be taken in and "digested." Taking in and processing impressions is just as important for the soul's survival as taking in and processing food is for the survival of the physical body.

The main reason the body can maintain and regenerate is because it is given food which can be transformed within it. The etheric formative forces that are bonded with food substances are released through the life processes of nourishing and secreting, and made available to a human being's etheric body. (The fact that there are [or will be] individuals who can do without physical nourishment and feed themselves with regenerating, living etheric forces is a subject that will not be dealt with here.)

Likewise, the development of our soul depends upon the impressions it is allowed to have. If a human soul repeatedly receives varied and valuable impressions from all twelve areas of the senses, then it will be accordingly many-faceted because it has access to a broader field of experience upon which it can develop perceptions.

Adequate soul nourishment gives rise to the capacity for perception, a broad field of soul experience, and the associated possibilities for flexible, wide-ranging thinking and willing. In early childhood soul nourishment first and foremost involves sensory experiences that are meaningful and comprehensible to children, so that they do not lead to overstimulation. This always requires subsequent rest periods to "digest." Other important food for the soul is added in later childhood, youth, and adulthood. In order to be properly nourished and develop a wide spectrum of sensory experience, the soul requires intense immersion into the realm of perception and increased efforts of will. After puberty, increased intellectual challenges as well as practice in developing powers of judgment become appropriate.

If such "nourishment" is missing, then in a certain way the soul remains poor. If the soul is over-stimulated with too many impressions it will "spit" them back out again by way of impulsive comments and movements (often seen in over-stimulated children). Or impressions may remain undigested and become a burden to the soul, which will negatively affect the life of feeling and general sense of well-being (often seen in over-stimulated adults and, unfortunately, more and more in children as well).

As for nourishment of the spirit, it can be said that intellectual subject matter, real knowledge, or having a connection to an ideal are gifts of the nourishing soul to the spirit. The spiritual intake is actually a broadening of individual experience and can no longer be lost. That is the reason it is so important to have the life process of nourishing well-anchored in the physical and soul aspects, so that a healthy body will be able to accommodate a wide variety of soul experiences which the spirit can then receive for its nourishment and enrichment.

After death, first the physical body and then the structure of etheric forces fall away from the spirit, and later, the constitution of the soul. What remains is that which has been imparted to the immortal spirit and never dies, but is brought into a future incarnation as potential abilities (See Steiner, *Theosophy*, Chapter 2, GA 9).

To summarize: Just as nourishment taken into the physical body can be broken down only by secreted substances (saliva, gastric acid, pancreatic secretions), so it is with the soul-spirit element; what is taken in can be deconstructed and assessed without prejudice only if analysis of the "soul nourishment" takes place through perception and experience. Without the ability to *analyze,* no sensory impression, no experience of emotion and no intellectual subject matter can be "digested" in a healthy way. Everyone has experienced feeling overwhelmed by emotion. It is not negative, as such. However, it can be observed that this always happens when no analytical examination of the emotional feelings has taken place; that is to say, the formation of the concept is not complete. If there is a situation where a flood of emotions causes stress, interestingly, it can result in over-acidity in the stomach and occasionally heartburn or even a stomach ulcer. Here we can clearly see there is also a connection between body and soul as it relates to the life process of nourishing; thus we have such sayings as "It felt like a punch in the stomach" or "I'm feeling sour."

Integration of the Nourishing Process during the First Seven Years and Its Transformation

After birth a newborn's metabolic system is still too immature to allow for any food intake. As a matter of fact, nature has arranged it so that a mother's milk does not "come in" for two or three days after the birth. Until then, a newborn baby is nourished by a few drops of the colostrum milk, which has a high fat content, and the layer of fat under its skin. Only afterward does an infant begin to drink larger amounts of breast milk. However, for a few months, often after breastfeeding, the baby may spit up part of the milk. If breastfeeding is not possible, the replacement formula has to be sweet and relatively diluted, using boiled water, so that the baby will be able to tolerate the milk formula. Sometimes when cow's milk is given too soon, a baby may develop an allergy. If alternatives are lacking, one could try using milk from a mare or donkey with thinned almond butter. One notices right away that nourishment has to be studied a long time before it "works."

The next steps are to introduce puréed fruits and vegetables, slightly more solid milk porridges, bread to be gummed, or chewed if there are teeth, the first crackers, and so on. Over the course of the first two years, the need to prepare special foods exclusively for the child gradually lessens. Eventually, the whole family is able to eat the same things as long as foods are cut up into manageable bites for the child because of still-missing molars.

On the way to a normal diet, from an adult's perspective, the slightest excess can lead to digestive disturbances. Just one spoonful too many of puréed carrots can cause days of constipation; citrus fruits may lead to painful diaper rash. This is likewise an indication that the secreting process is not yet able to deal effectively with the food on offer.

At the *soul* level, children of one or two years of age are able to receive only those sensory experiences and occupy themselves only with such things as are in their field of vision. They are a long way from being able to play an imaginative game, feel an inner connection to an object, or understand everything spoken in their surroundings.

However, the more the nourishing life process becomes anchored in the physical body during the first seven years, and the intake and mechanical and chemical breaking down of foods with complex proteins and fats becomes more efficient, the better a child is able to make soul connections with the world. During the course of the fourth year these emotional connections find their way into imaginative play.

At eighteen months to two years of age, a child is able to play with something for hardly more than a minute, but kindergartners, at age four to five, can play for considerably longer periods of time. In the sixth and seventh years, in connection with the developing capabilities of concentration and enthusiasm, children will increasingly be able to *connect* with some specific type of play for a period of days and are also gradually more successful in understanding words spoken to them by adults.

The younger a child, the more we see how things that come at the child by way of sensory impressions have to be "spit out" again through movement or speech. Just as there is less tolerance for foods that are hard to digest, such as fatty meat, fish, egg dishes, or whole-grain dishes that are not pre-processed enough in the toddler years, similarly, the soul is not able to completely receive all the impressions. In the first few years of life when a child is confronted with an impression, the soul reacts immediately. Either the whole body moves, clear down to the toes, when something is tasted or heard, or immediate comments are made about something whizzing by: "There! Car! Look! There! Bus! Vroom!"

When a child is kindergarten age, relationships to the things in life that quickly pass by the soul begin to change. From the way things like a beginning rain shower, a bird flying by, a story, a puppet play, a word, and so on, are completely taken into the soul, it can be determined to what extent the nourishment life process is already anchored in the physical body and the forces required for the soul to receive things have been released.

In the sixth and seventh years children exhibit not only the ability to receive and accept things, but also the beginnings of the ability to make an inner connection with something. In the previous chapters on breathing and warming, we spoke about the development of the faculties of concentration and enthusiasm when a child is ready for school. Likewise, with the development of the nourishing life process we can speak about the unfolding of the ability to make inner connections. This continues to the point where more intensive friendships develop. Furthermore, with the release of the forces associated with the nourishing process, a child may now make a connection with subject matter presented by a well-loved adult; a connection is created from "I" to you, in preparation for the transition from implicit to explicit learning. This is a very important step on the path to the experiential world of the second seven-year stage, where learning is facilitated by imagination, music, and art. Soul faculties such as attention, concentration, and enthusiasm are not enough for a soul to be able to receive things of the world. A child also needs the ability to make real soul connections so that something remains which can then be processed, sorted, and (especially important) remembered.

Another result of the partial release of the life processes of nourishing and secreting from their purely physical orientation is the ability to deconstruct; that is to say, a kind of soul-oriented dissection process is discovered. However, this ability first appears with puberty. The birth of the astral body means that a young person steps onto the world stage, also in the sense of the soul and spirit. The influence of the environment on one's own self is usually experienced as something embarrassing, and practicing one's own free will and judgment, without regard for convention and authority, steps into the foreground. This ability cannot yet appear during the transition from kindergarten-age to school-age, even though it is the result of a release of forces in the nourishing process. First of all, the emulation of self-chosen and loved authority figures, which is now slowly overshadowing the ability to imitate, would never allow such a faculty as skepticism to exist, and, second, the ability for analytical thought that comes out of the secreting process is released only after puberty. In the soul-spirit aspect, the ability for analytical thought forms the same relationship to such a dissection process as the secreted gastric acid does to the nourishing process of disintegration in the physical body.

Children with less stable social bonds, and therefore a lack of love for authority figures, examine and assess experiences already in early school-age. These are then able to be deconstructed with an attitude of skepticism, as is normally the case only after puberty, because the faculty of analytical thinking has been released from the secreting process too early. Normally, this will have a disastrous effect on schooling because the ability to make an inner connection with the subject matter as a result of forces being released from the nourishment life process is fully overshadowed by the possibility of examining things in an analytical way. "What do I need this for?" becomes an expression of critical skepticism residing in the soul. The drive to exercise one's own faculty of judgment before puberty stands in the way of forming an inner connection with the world for one's own enrichment.

Secreting

The life process of secreting has to do with all the "organizing" and "sorting" that takes place in the physical organism. All elimination processes, as well as the secretions of sweat glands, pancreas, or stomach (in the form of gastric acid), belong in this category. The diffusion of neurotransmitters between two nerve fibers and the exhalation of carbon dioxide are also part of the secretion process. Since a strict separation of the seven life processes is only possible intellectually, it is important to point out that the *formation* of sweat, saliva, or gastric acid is actually a process of production that belongs with the *producing – reproducing* life process, while the *release* of these secretions is a process of secretion. The formation of the substance is for the purpose of secretion.

As it relates to physical metabolic activity, the cooperation between the processes of nourishing and secreting has already been highlighted in the chapter on nourishing.

In contrast to the actions of intake, combining together, and disintegration (*nourishing*), secreting includes everything that happens during the disintegration and utilization of food substances; secretion to the inside and elimination to the outside. This is an internal organizational process, a process of analysis.

Therefore, the internal, organizing secretion process is the fourth and not the third life process because, to take digestion as an example, from a functional viewpoint something first has to be ingested before secretions in the form of saliva, gastric acid, and so on can come into play and be analyzed and sorted — even though the two processes largely take place at the same time. The production and secretion of saliva happen *as a result of* combining different foods in the cooking pot, on the plate, and in the mouth, even though saliva actually flows before any eating takes place. Nourishing is therefore a precondition for secreting.

Aside from those immediately involved in digestion, processes of secretion are always occurring throughout the entire body. For instance, dead blood cells are continually filtered out of our bloodstream and sent to the liver, which uses them to produce the bile necessary for digestion, demonstrating cooperation between the secreting process and the maintaining process.

The secreting process is, in turn, the precondition for the life process of maintaining. Without a new ordering of the substances that are taken in, and without a process of analysis, which keeps what is necessary and eliminates what is superfluous, no physical process of maintaining can be successful because otherwise the substances needed for regeneration would be missing.

Physical Secretion

When we eat food, the first process of secretion that takes place is the secretion of saliva. Further along in the process, the release of gastric acid, insulin, and glucagon occurs; then later, in the intestinal tract, there is a release of pancreatic secretions and bile. These are the secretions necessary to process the masticated food and make it possible to fully break down the food substances. Up to this point nourishing and secreting are closely connected.

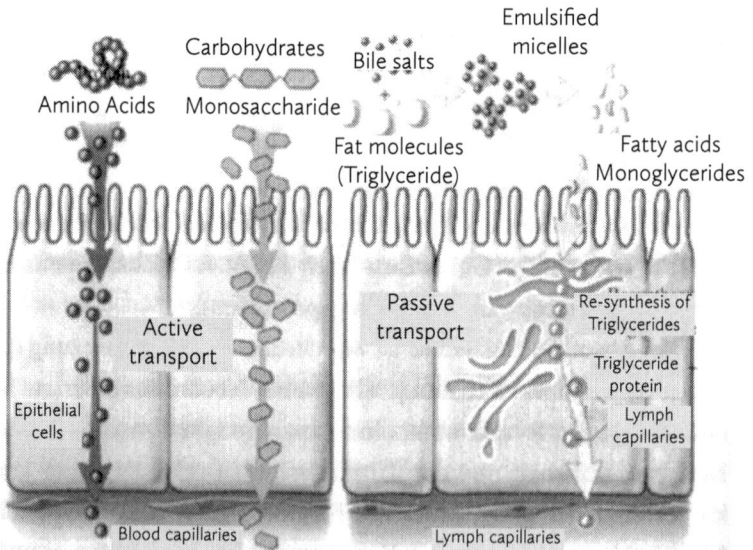

FIGURE 10

The absorption of split-apart and broken-down substances through the wall of the small intestine.

Source: http://www.zum.de/Faecher/Materialien/beck/chemcurs/12/cs12-55.htm

Now the secretion process in the small intestine clearly assumes control. Provided there has been adequate breaking down of the food substances, "energetic sorting" takes place in the small intestine. The fat molecules, chemically split apart by saliva, gastric acid, and pancreatic secretions, are now monoglycerides (the simplest form of fat) and free fatty acids, among other things. They combine with bile salts secreted into the intestinal tract by the gallbladder to form micelles, which are absorbed through the wall of the small intestine with the help of the villi, tiny hair-like appendages lining the intestinal wall. After absorption through the intestinal wall the released fat molecules are mostly taken into the lymphatic vessels, but also partly into the bloodstream. Something similar can be seen with the split carbohydrate and protein molecules. By going through the mouth, stomach, duodenum and small intestine they split apart and form monosaccharides (the simplest form of sugar) and amino acids (the simplest protein structure) in order to be absorbed through the intestinal wall (see Figure 10).

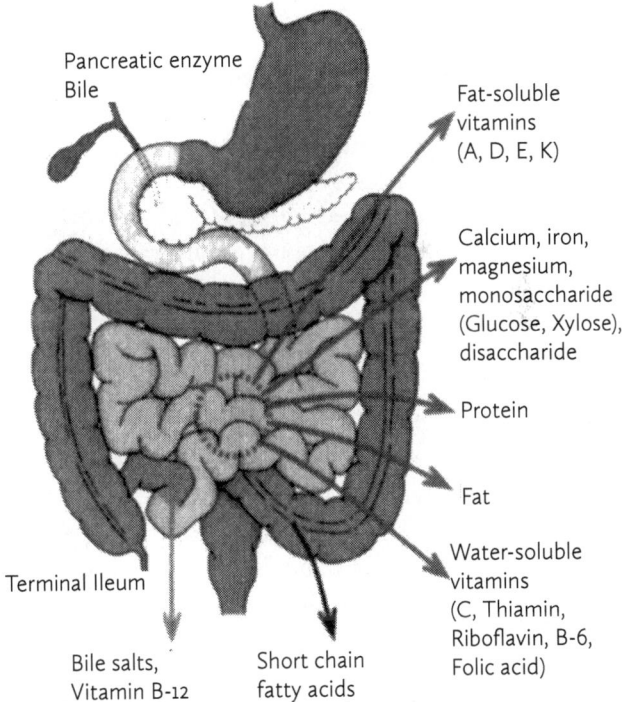

FIGURE 11

Places where internal secretion and utilization processes happen.

Source: Renz-Polster and Krautzig, 2008

In connection with the physical sorting of substances that have been split apart and broken down, it is interesting to discover that the breaking-down (digestion) and absorption of various substances to the inside (assimilation) happen partially in different places. For example, fat, protein, sugar, vitamin C, Vitamin A, folic acid, calcium, iron, and magnesium can be absorbed along the whole length of the small intestine. However, in the case of vitamin B-12, for example, this happens only at the end of the small intestine, and with short-chain fatty acids, the process takes place in the large intestine (see Figure 11).

Everything that is left over, that cannot be internally absorbed, remains in the colon and is then eliminated. For instance, it may happen that the fat contained in a very fat-rich meal cannot be completely split up into monoglycerides, so they remain in the colon as more complex fat molecules (diglycerides, triglycerides).

The views of natural science could be broadened by applying anthroposophical knowledge of human beings. With the help of the secreting process, matter is dissolved to the point where only the possibility of it remains, a kind of substance potency (a term used in homeopathy referring to the dilution of substances), which is the same as saying that only the idea of the substance remains. This is where real material transformation happens. The information contained in the substance leads to formative forces structuring completely new substances of their own. It is clear that the remaining life processes of maintaining, growing, and producing – reproducing must work together here. With the secreting process one recognizes that internalization, turning something from the outside to the inside, is taking place.

Other processes of secretion are found in the activities of the spleen, kidneys, and bladder. While the spleen, among other things, helps to eliminate old red blood cells (Jürgens, 2004), the special function of the kidneys is to break down substances that are no longer needed. There is a constant flow of blood to the kidneys where the metabolic waste products in the blood are filtered out. This is a very remarkable sorting and organizational process in the body. The kidneys produce about 120 ml of primary urine per minute from the blood flowing through them (about 170 liters per day). Toxins, electrolytes and uric acid (a waste product of protein metabolism) are filtered out of the primary urine and, for the most part, the filtered liquid goes back into the bloodstream (Juergens, 2004). The body's entire volume of blood passes through the filtering function of the kidneys about three times per hour. A small amount of the liquid containing the filtered-out substances remains and flows into the bladder as urine and is then eliminated several times a day by urination (about 1.5 liters per day for adults).

Secretion processes are involved in other things besides the utilization of nutrients and cleaning the blood. Secretion is also involved in the processing of sensory stimuli.

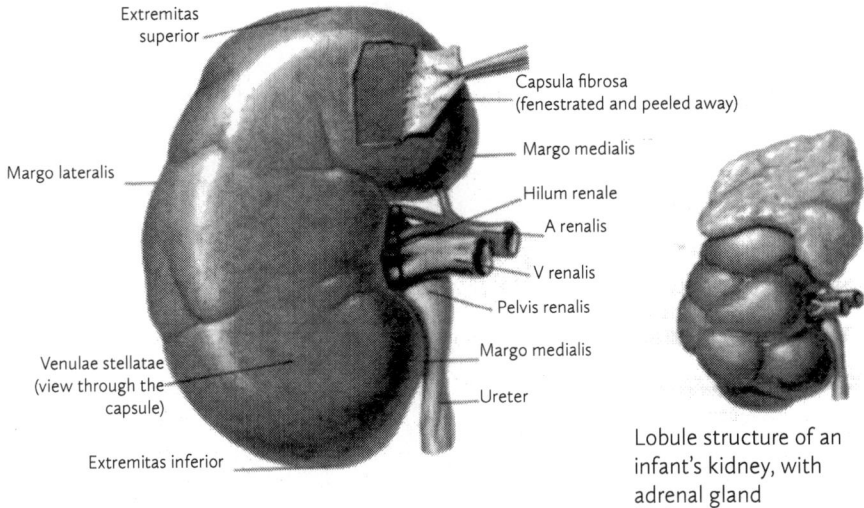

Extremitas superior

Capsula fibrosa (fenestrated and peeled away)

Margo medialis

Hilum renale

A renalis

V renalis

Pelvis renalis

Margo medialis

Ureter

Margo lateralis

Venulae stellatae (view through the capsule)

Extremitas inferior

Lobule structure of an infant's kidney, with adrenal gland

FIGURE 12

Human kidney.

Source: Netter, 2008

A sensory stimulus travels as an electrical impulse via a nerve pathway to the brain. There, the following process takes place: In most cases the nerve pathway ends with a presynaptic nerve ending. Neurotransmitters are released from the thickened nerve ending (similar to the secretion process in a gland) whereby the previous electrical impulse goes over the synaptic cleft to the opposite nerve ending (postsynaptic nerve ending) as a chemical impulse. There, the incoming chemical impulse is recognized and changed back into an electrical impulse.

The secreting process is most clearly recognizable if we examine visual perception.

If one sees a ball, for instance, the perception is sent into the field of vision where it is analyzed and categorized so that the perceptions of form, color, distance, surface quality, and so on can be sent on to different areas of the brain. The "I" has to produce the synthesis "ball" from out of a great variety of perceptions, which means that at every moment I am the creator of my own world!

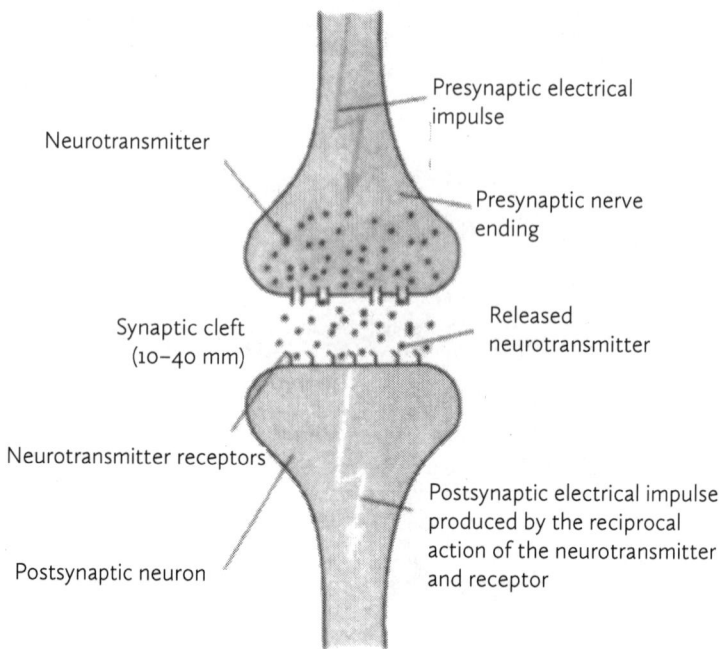

FIGURE 13

Diagram of a synaptic transfer.

Source: http://www.onmeda.de/aktuelles/themenspecial/gesund_durch_den_winter/depressive_verstimmungen-ursachen-15638-3.html

The above description of how a sensory impression is deconstructed through the transformation of an electrical nerve impulse into a chemical state, and the resultant reprocessing and integration with previous sensory experiences, makes it clear that the life process of secreting is really precisely in the middle, between the life processes that make it possible to receive the world (breathing, warming, nourishing), and the life processes through which something new is integrated into the world (maintaining, growing, producing – reproducing).

Every sensory impression is first "tasted" through breathing and accepted with more or less intensity. It is met with a certain amount of interest and warming, without which no living nerve impulse would be possible. It is ingested like nourishment; that is, processed, and with the help of secretions, it is split apart. Then the deconstructed sensory impulse is put back together using the formative forces of the "I" that are not bound to the physical body. It does not get lost in the subconscious, but is held by the "I" and can therefore be remembered and enrich previous experiences of the soul. This leads to growth in the number of neural connections in the brain, increasing richness of soul and allowing for the emergence of ideas that can only result from a wealth of experience. Without impressions of sound it would be impossible to compose a piece of music, and without knowledge of color it would be impossible to realize an artistic concept of the relationship between blue and yellow through a variety of differentiated greens.

The same can be observed with food intake, as previously described. Substances are taken from the external world and, after they have gone through the seven life processes, are reintegrated into the world as newly configured substances.

Food is first perceived through breathing. It is smelled, viewed (food is served to look appealing, for example), and some warmth production occurs. The mouth and stomach need a certain amount of heat in order to function, and without some interest in eating, warmth production will not take place. The food is ingested and broken down into its chemical components. There is nothing left of the original food. With the help of analyzing secretions, the "I" decides what will become of the components. One component will be given to the life process of maintaining for regeneration of the physical body, and another will be eliminated from the body. The remaining substances have now been newly formed by the "I" and have never before been in the world. Through this new formation, regeneration can now proceed and growth and reproduction can begin.

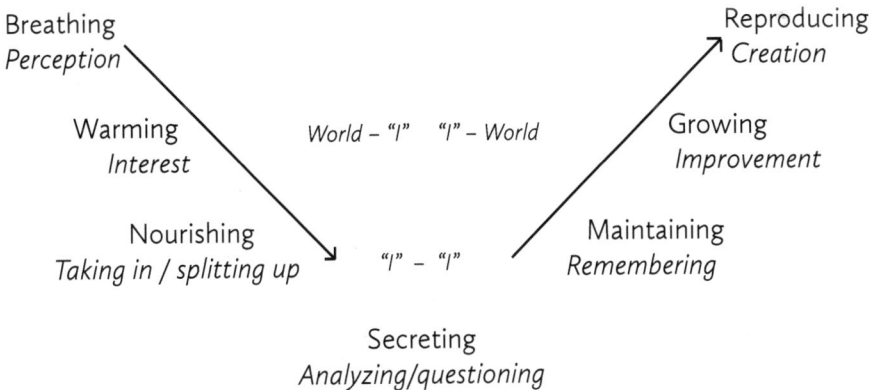

Breathing
Perception

Reproducing
Creation

Warming
Interest

World – "I"   "I" – World

Growing
Improvement

Nourishing
Taking in / splitting up

"I" – "I"

Maintaining
Remembering

Secreting
Analyzing/questioning

What has thus been formed in the human organism is truly a new creation. The human being presents a newly formed physical body to the world which has nothing more to do with its earlier material composition or with the ingested food.

In the secreting process there is constant contact between material substance and spirit, which determines the new form of the substance, even though this does not happen consciously in the processing of nourishment and sensory impressions. As will be shown, in the secretion processes of the soul and spirit, the contact that the "I" has with what has been given becomes somewhat clearer and more conscious through the process of sorting and analyzing. In an untranslated lecture (GA 343), Steiner says:

> External matter is transformed within us. And what happens to it? It becomes something of spirit within us. What is usually not realized is that a human being, through the digestive process, actually enters into the transformation of the external world up to the spiritualization of external material processes. In the external world it is actually world processes that are playing out. World processes are playing out in fragments until, let us say, grain is produced and other things that are used for food. That which is produced in the external world will be transformed for the first time within a human being. Through the transformation process, it is on its way to the spirit element. It cannot change into something with a spirit nature in the physical, external world, but only inside a human being. This is simply an objective fact that I am relating here, nothing else.

This is actually the archetypal image of transubstantiation; changing bread and wine into the body and blood of Christ. Steiner further says in the same lecture:

> If one wishes to place the transformation process before humanity so that it will be looked upon the same as the external world is looked upon, then one has to place something in the external world that otherwise does not occur there, but only plays out within a human being. For this reason, a sacramental act was placed into the world; something that does not occur in nature, but plays out in human beings as the secret of humanity. If one wishes to place before humanity that which belongs to their innermost being, as we have just characterized it, then one has the transformation of bread and wine into the body and blood of Christ; one has the transubstantiation. The transubstantiation is not a discovery made in the external world. It is placing before the external world that which, in reality, occurs in the deepest recesses of a human being.

In the fifth lecture of the series titled *An Occult Physiology* (GA 128), Rudolf Steiner explains that the secreting processes are the fundamental requirement for self-awareness and therefore are of decisive importance for a person's relationship to self:

> *Let us suppose that the human organism takes into itself, into one of its organs, the stomach, for instance, a certain material substance, and that this organ system is designed, through its own activity, to eliminate something from the substance taken in, take something away from the totality of the substance, so that, through the action of the organ, the substance, as a totality, is split apart into a finer, quasi-filtered part and a coarser part that will be excreted. Thus a differentiation of the substance has been undertaken. One part is transformed into a substance that will be of further use and which other organs will be able to receive. The other part is first separated out and then excreted. Here, where the unuseable part of the material substance is repelled from the useable part, you have a modified version of a situation similar to running into something; some external object... In a manner of speaking, when the ingested substance-stream comes to an organ it meets resistance; it cannot remain as it is, it must change. It is as if the organ was saying: "You cannot stay like this, the way you are, you have to change." Resistance is put in the way of the substance. It must be further utilized as a different substance and it has to eliminate certain parts. Inside our bodies, an organ positions itself against the stream of substance in the same way some external object is positioned against us when we run into it. Such resistances are found within the entire physical organism in a great many organs.*
>
> *Through the fact that secretions take place in our physical organism and that we have organs of secretion; that is the only reason we have the possibility of a whole organism that is a self-contained and self-experiencing being. Only a being that meets up with resistance is able to have experience.*

In relation to this, one can also see that when a young child between the age of two-and-one-half to three years awakens to the genital area and perceives his or her own sex, and when motor function has progressed to the point where there is self-control of the sphincter muscles, then the need for cleanliness in the genital area develops naturally from within the child. Perception of the self in one's own body as "I," which is easily identified during the "terrible twos" phase, happens because of a child's own developmental impulse, and likewise with the need to accomplish processes of elimination and excretion just like the "big kids."

This explains *one* connection between physical processes and soul-spirit experiences, which leads us to the next consideration about the secreting process.

Soul-Spirit Secretion Capability

One of the quotations above spoke about how the physical secreting processes make possible the perception of self. Now, the secreting process as it relates to the soul will be presented as a process of the soul. The physical body is not the only aspect of a human being that secretes, sorts, keeps, and so forth. The soul also organizes and analyzes in order to bring structure into the fullness of perceptions and impressions.

Sense *perceptions* are constantly flowing into the soul from the physical body, interrupted only by sleep. For the life of the soul, this also means that *sensations* are constantly appearing before it. Perceptions resulting in sensations are made possible by the living functions of the etheric body; in other words, they are made possible by the presence of the seven life processes. The sense perceptions that flow toward us, which were spoken about in the chapter on nourishing, are necessary for the soul's survival, but they have to be categorized. This is a soul process which protects against every sense perception being considered equally important. Irrespective of any objective criteria, the soul constantly sorts and categorizes according to what seems important or unimportant. If this were not the case, we would suffer either from "diarrhea" of the soul (not caring about anything) or "constipation" of the soul (a compulsion to keep everything, every little thing seems important). Finding the right balance between acceptance and rejection has a healthy effect on the soul and shows how well the soul aspect of the secreting process is functioning.

The fact that tension in the soul can lead to physical constipation shows another connection between the physical and soul aspects, as they relate to the secretion life process, besides the perception of self. A good example of this would be how difficult it is to deal with all the new and unfamiliar impressions one experiences while traveling.

It has been said with regard to the contact the "I" has with the split-apart substances resulting from taking in nourishment, or the deconstructed nerve impulses resulting from a sensory impulse, that such contact between spirit and matter remains at an unconscious level. But the sorting and categorizing that takes place in the soul is a little more conscious. It is not yet at the level of waking consciousness, but rather more like dream-consciousness. The decision to categorize the rattling streetcar in the background as not having the same importance as a whispered conversation with someone sitting across from you is the result of becoming used to the constant presence of the streetcar, and not a conscious decision to ignore it. If you stand in a forest, for example, in which the trees are rustling and there is a bubbling brook with birds singing, then you have a chance to practice the soul's capability of deciding what to accept and what to ignore by alternating between allowing first one and then the other sensory perception to enter your soul. Here again, the connection between all the life processes is apparent because consciously paying attention, or not paying attention, cannot be done without concentrated perception (breathing), interest (warming), and the ability to take something in (nourishing).

When it comes to sorting and categorizing *thoughts*, the secreting process is completely conscious. In this case it does not have to do with familiar patterns of acceptance or ignoring certain sensory perceptions; it has to do with thoughts helping the "I" with its analytical activity. When analysis takes place, when levels of thought are differentiated, something is thoroughly investigated and the "I" consciously judges if it is of concern to the intellect; that is a conscious secreting process. The ability to examine things analytically prevents our being overwhelmed with feelings and emotions, as was previously discussed (in the section "Integration of the Nourishing Process during the First Seven Years and Its Transformation"). The secreting process in thinking is the only thing that can bring enlightenment and clarity to such situations.

Through unconscious physical processes of secretion, physical health and the possibility of experiencing the self are created. Soul-secretions produce feelings of well-being and a sense of being guided, but these take place in a dream-like state of consciousness. Secretions taking place in a state of wakeful consciousness produce clarity.

Integration of the Secreting Process during the First Seven Years and Its Transformation

When a child first enters the world, he is overwhelmed by sensory impressions. In the first few weeks of life there are perceptions of touch from lying down, wearing clothing, and the touch of parents and caregivers. There is also the perception of hunger, which involves a sense for life and survival, but also the perception of motion, such as kicking, and, further, perceptions of maintaining balance, cold, heat, noises, and gradually also color. All of these things are coming at a child as perceptions, but there has been no chance to form any kind of internal organization of all the experiences.

As a child becomes older the experiences from the realm of the twelve senses become much more varied. Crawling babies have more experiences of touch, taste, and self-propelled motion. During the toddler years there are more perceptions having to do with words, thoughts, and the "I"-sense. However, these perceptions would be just a "mish-mash of experiences" without having some kind of internal organization. For this reason, very young children may call everything that is round-shaped a "ball" and all men "Papa," for example.

Taking in unsorted perceptions in this way is connected to the as yet inadequate anchoring of the life process of secreting during the first few years of life. This process, like all the others, has to slowly find its way into the physical body. One way this can be recognized is through the fact that it takes a number of years for bowel movements to take the form that will be maintained for the rest of a person's life, except during periods of illness. With very young children it is fairly easy to tell what has been eaten by looking at their bowel movements; especially before they are one year old. This means that the inner secreting processes involving gastric acid, pancreas secretions, and bile are not yet capable of causing transformation of substances to the same degree as is the case later on.

Bowel movements are not the only things pointing to the fact that the secreting processes are not yet properly anchored in the physical body; there is also a somewhat uncontrolled saliva production and an inability to properly regulate the sweat process in the first year of life.

Gradual integration of the secreting process becomes more visible when a child reaches kindergarten age. Drooling decreases, sweating is better regulated, and bowel movements become more regular and their appearance is less affected by the food consumed. Beginning around age three, children start to ask more questions. It is like an awakening to the idea of correctly distinguishing things from each other. A child is not especially interested in lengthy explanations from an adult, but rather intensively experiences the idea of "questioning."

Along with the increase in internal, bodily processes of sorting and categorizing in the third, fourth, and fifth years, an ability to sort and organize things in the surroundings begins to emerge. At home or in the kindergarten, chestnut goes with chestnut, and pinecone with pinecone; we may also observe more refined organizational processes such as sorting dolls according to size, or towels according to color.

The soul's emerging capacity for sorting and organizing is the result of an anchoring of the secreting life process. That is to say, wherever secreting already "functions," the forces which brought the secreting function into the physical body are now freed for activities of the soul.

It is interesting to observe that those children who have loosely formed bowel movements, and have to wipe their bottoms more because of it, often muddle up one thing or the other relating to their soul experiences. The inability to produce "orderly" excretions correlates with a lack of order in the soul. Physical and soul aspects are always mixed up together.

In the sixth and seventh years, when this ability to arrange and classify is possible in a somewhat larger context, such as arranging an entire room or putting songs in order according to the seasons, it shows a strong connection of the secreting processes with the physical body, resulting in a lot of sorting and ordering capabilities being freed up for the soul element. Then the "big kids" in the kindergarten are the ones who are sure to know the right place for every little thing in the kindergarten and are able to tidy up things very well. Regardless of whether a child enjoys tidying up or not, the ability to do it indicates that school readiness is not far off.

Another aspect of being able to correctly sort and order things is that it allows children to have a lot of fun playing around with the concept. For instance, it is very funny to sing Christmas songs in the summer, or "upside-down world" might become their favorite game.

A further characteristic of an increasingly outwardly-expressed secretion process in the soul is the absolute rejection of a situation or a food. While three-year-olds can usually still be persuaded to sing or paint or try a certain food, such tactics of persuasion really do not work any more with six-year-olds.

The capacity to distinguish things, sort, organize, and relatively firmly reject something is the result of the integration of the secreting life process into the physical body. If it is successful, the forces produced through the anchoring process are now free for soul activities, and the child is ready for school.

This ordering process that has become part of the soul gives the possibility of analytical thought, which leads to very individual questions and subjective judgments. However, these capacities are released only after puberty, when the things of the world rise up into a youth's soul as emotionally significant experiences, calling forth an inner position, opinion, or response. In the first years of school, children only use their soul capacity for sorting and ordering in relation to things which a well-loved authority figure tells them about the world. Letters, numbers, stories about plants, animals, and so on, are all meaningfully arranged and integrated into previous experiences. When a child reaches puberty, because of the birth of the astral body, there is an increase in autonomous questioning of the conditions in the world, whereby, increasingly, the capacity for analysis and subjective judgment are used to skeptically deconstruct happenings in the world; that is, to dissect on a soul-spirit level, comparable to what happens during the nourishing process.

Taking these things into consideration, it is easy to see how weakening it is when early questioning is seen by our present educational system as an opportunity to intellectually dissect world conditions. Before puberty a child is searching for a connection between the "I" and the world and an experience of coherency. If the faculty of analysis is brought out too soon, then the physical body will be missing the formative forces needed for transformation.

To once more highlight the connection between nutrition and secretion relative to the physical and soul-spirit aspects, the importance of secretions to the nourishment process should again be pointed out. The physical secretions (saliva, gastric acid, etc.) make physical nourishment possible; that is, chemical splitting of food substances. The soul faculties which result from the release of the secreting life processes from their purely physical orientation (ordering, sorting, rejecting) make soul nourishment possible; that is, taking in and making an inner connection with things in the surroundings. The soul-spirit faculties of analysis, questioning, and subjective judgment which result from the secretion processes after puberty (if there is healthy development) make spiritual nourishment possible; that is, taking in and making an inner connection with laws, principles and ideals contained in the immortal, spiritual core of a human being.

Maintaining

The life process that follows nourishing and secreting is the process we may name "maintaining." The processes already described are a precondition for the process of maintaining: Without breathing, functioning warmth production, and successful metabolism relating to nourishment and secretion, no form or function can be maintained or preserved. Since growth and reproduction are necessary to such maintenance, it becomes increasingly more difficult to think of the individual processes as separate from one another. Besides the physical aspects, there are also soul-spirit aspects observable in the life process of maintaining. First of all, we will take a look at the effects of this life process as it relates to the physical body.

Physical Maintenance

The physical body is continuously maintained and regenerated. With very few exceptions, all the cells in the body are replaced with new cells after a certain period of time (reproduction).

The various types of cells in the body have differing life spans. Here are a few examples (Kunsch and Kunsch, 2006):

Cell Type:	Lifespan:
Small Intestine Cells	1 – 2 days
Stomach Lining	About 1 week
Lung Surface	8 days
Colon Cells	10 days
Skin Cells	Average of 4 weeks
Olfactory Cells in the Nose	1 – 2 months
Red Blood Cells	About 4 months
Bone Cells	10 years (Longer for the elderly)

But even the non-renewable cells found inside the eyes, ears, heart muscle, or hair follicles are provided with new substances and are therefore refreshed from the inside (Buchta, Höper and Sönnichsen, 2006).

If an outer substance is given to the physical body in the form of nourishment and is then made available to the body as a transformed substance by way of secretion processes in the mouth, stomach, and duodenum, and the sorting and elimination processes in the small and large intestines, the life process of maintaining is able to unfold. This process is served not by the substances that are eliminated through the intestines or the kidneys and bladder, but by those that are kept. The last three phases of metabolism are the ones that play into the life processes of nourishing, secreting and maintaining.

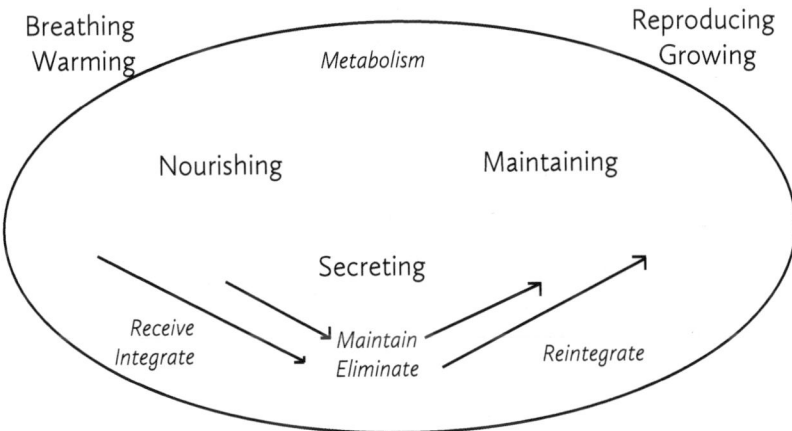

Physical body forms and organ functions have to be constantly maintained and regenerated. This is achieved by the steady renewal of physical matter by the substances that are separated out from nourishment. However, the maintaining process is also served by the reception and formation of substances from air and light.

The skin is renewed unceasingly and therefore its function is maintained. Old skin cells are sloughed off the skin's surface and fall away. Bones and organs are constantly renewed and therefore maintained. A burn on the tongue is healed within hours, and even deep wounds or broken bones grow back together. There are many other examples of the maintaining of the physical body and its living functions.

Here are a few examples to show the power of the maintaining process and its pervasiveness throughout the physical body:

Certain substances such as calcium or phosphate are dissolved out of the food consumed and always used for renewing bones. New cells are continually formed inside the bones which replace the old outer cells. The physical organism produces osteoblasts, which contribute to the formation of new bone tissue, as well as osteoclasts, which break down old bone tissue cells. Our understanding today is that in children and young adults all the bones are completely renewed every ten years, but with increasing age this can be slowed considerably, resulting in older, more porous bones and perhaps even osteoporosis. The chemical processes inside the body which lead to new bone tissue formation are highly complex. New bone tissue formation requires many different substances. Besides phosphates and hydrogen, the formation of calcium molecules is most decisive because it provides the mineral content of the bones. The mechanical demands made on the bones also play a significant role. With no load placed upon them, the bones would slowly crumble (Schmidt and Lang, 2007). *If children did not move constantly, they would not be able to form the bones they need later.*

Complex chemical processes facilitate localized inflammation of damaged tissue — on the skin or in a muscle, for example. This calls forth white blood cells (leukocytes), which are able to pass through blood vessel walls, go to the place where there is inflammation, and provide a certain protein for defense against germs and bacteria. In this way the organism is protected and cell division is stimulated until the wound is covered in new cells (Schmidt and Lang, 2007).

Rhodopsin, so-called visual purple, is a chemical pigment found in the rods of the retina, which is destroyed by exposure to light. Through vitamin A, among other things, the released chemical molecules are constantly re-synthesized back into rhodopsin so that the requirement for visual purple is always met by the body itself. An acute vitamin A deficiency is the only thing that could stand in the way of this process (Schneemann and Wurm, 1995).

These three examples clearly show how diligently the maintaining and regenerating processes are deployed in the body.

On the one hand, the maintaining process requires the results of the previous processes of nourishing and secreting in order to have at its disposal such things as calcium for the bones or vitamin A for the retinas. On the other hand, processes that support maintenance are also not possible without growth and production – reproduction. When there is a wound to be healed, it happens under the influence of the maintaining life process, but this requires the *production* of lymph and white blood cells as well as *growth* in the damaged tissue area through cell division in order to bring about successful regeneration.

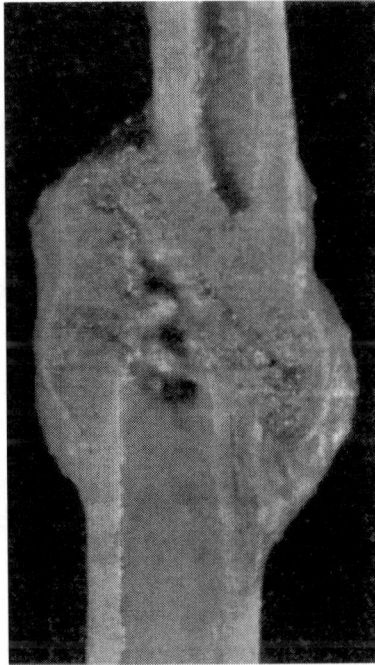

FIGURE 14

Example of maintaining skeletal function through callus formation after a broken bone.

Source: http://www.alt.med-rz.uniklinik-saarland.de/pathologie/Knochen_Pathologies?Text%20ofiles/Knochen_Path_3VII.htm

It is the same with maintaining bone matter, skin or organs: The maintaining process preserves and regenerates, but it requires cell division, which is a result of the growing process, and formation of specific substances connected with the producing – reproducing life process in order to function.

With that being said, the previous diagram has to be expanded as follows:

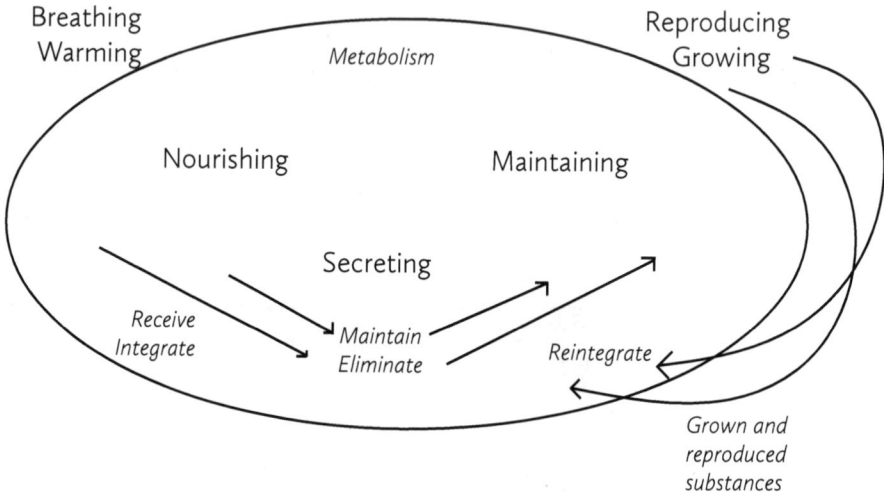

A further aspect of the maintaining process can be observed if we turn our attention to the continual preservation of blood in the body. Many reproduction processes within the body help maintain blood. However, clearly, the primary process for blood preservation is that of the air sacs in the lungs giving off oxygen when air is inhaled. Red blood cells (erythrocytes) are able to form in the blood only in connection with oxygen and the help of iron, among other things (Schmidt and Lang, 2007).

The maintaining process is not only facilitated by air but also by light. Through exposure to ultraviolet light, mainly direct sunlight, vitamin D is produced in the skin, for the most part. Cholesterol from the liver is transported to the skin for this purpose. There, with the help of sunlight, it is transformed into vitamin D and finally transported to fatty tissue where it is stored. Strictly speaking, vitamin D is not a vitamin but a hormone. It is used to help move forward the production of bone cells because it influences calcium and phosphate metabolism (Schmidt and Lang, 2007). Bone cell formation, and with it the continual preservation of the bones facilitated by calcium and phosphate, is successful only because of the formation of vitamin D through ultraviolet light. If there is a vitamin D deficiency it can cause rickets, a bone disease that causes softening of the bones. Rickets is a risk in occupations where work takes place underground, like coal mining. It can lead to deformities in the ribcage, a so-called funnel chest (pectus excavatum), or bowed legs. The anthroposophical view on vitamin D supplementation for infants is one of criticism; however, the practice has mostly erased the danger of contracting rickets in Central Europe. On the rise are diseases which cause a tendency to hardening, such as sclerosis. Supplementing with vitamin D instead of getting enough outdoor exercise, especially during the time when the skeleton is trying to mold itself into its own, individual form, will have a deforming and hardening effect on the skeletal system.

On the whole, through the maintaining life process, the power of the forces of the etheric body is especially apparent. With the help of the seven life processes, the etheric forces are able to bring dead mineral substances and non-living elements such as carbon, hydrogen, oxygen, and nitrogen into a living, connecting form, and therefore into living functions.

Normally, this life process is also active in the preservation of a sensory impression. In the chapter on secretions it has already been pointed out how important the secreting process is to synaptic transfers of sensory impulses; that is, nerve impulses (see the section "Physical Secretion"). After an electrical nerve impulse has been transformed into a chemical potential, which the secreted neurotransmitter carries from the presynaptic nerve ending to the postsynaptic nerve ending, the now-approaching chemical impulse has to be changed back into an electrical potential and be reintegrated into the neuronal structure within the brain. That which approaches as an impulse has to be kept, just as a needed food substance has to be kept after ingestion. In principle, it could also be lost — not utilized and preserved, but excreted. The more often a sensory impulse is carried to the brain by way of synapses, the stronger the associated synapses become (Rüegg, 2007). There is a steadily increasing capability for preservation, and therefore also memory, of a specific sensory impulse, or rather, a complex group of related sensory perceptions. It would require more than one instance of simultaneous impressions, such as seeing and smelling a rose, in order for the soul to preserve the connection between different sensory impressions. The physical precondition for this is constantly repeated perceptions. This is the only way the synapses will become so strong, by way of a multitude of connections, that a real soul-experience can be gained from them.

With all of the life processes, it is important to take the pausing of activity into consideration. In the case of a young child one can observe that the child will try a new movement, repeat it, and then enjoy a pause before repeating the movement again. Within the pause is where a physical connection is made. For older children, sleep is a must after any learning and exercise activities — riding a bicycle or learning the vowels, for example. Understanding and comprehension go through changes during the night. The truth is, we learn in our sleep!

This is a very important consideration for healthy upbringing and education in the home, kindergarten, and school. Repetition and constant transformation of similar processes, as well as simultaneous perception of associated sensory impressions and adequate rest periods, strengthen the physical basis for correctly finding one's way into the world of the senses and recognizing phenomena in the world, which is beneficial for memory. If instead of simply putting bread on the table to eat, what if the flour is milled, the dough kneaded, and the whole house smells of bread baking, and then it is so hot that you have to be careful taking it in your hands? So many sense impressions would take place which, with repeated activity, would always be kept and reintegrated into the brain structure. Thus a highly complex network of different perceptions may unite to form a *significant relationship* and create a strong memory. Constantly maintaining and integrating such a complex of perceptions establishes the brain as the physical foundation of the soul for the faculties of thought and memory in an extraordinarily sophisticated way. It will become the physical foundation stone for understanding the connection between "I" and the world (coherency), and how discrete events in the world relate to each other.

Maintaining Processes of the Soul and Spirit

The physical body is not the only thing that maintains and regenerates its forms and functions, as well as sense impressions; the soul also preserves its content. Because of its coexistence with the etheric body, the physical body has the power to remember form and function. In contrast, the soul merely remembers its own soul-content. Just as the physical body maintains and regenerates ("remembers") the forms and functions of the nerves, senses, organ functions, and the musculoskeletal system, so are thoughts, feelings and emotions, and motion sequences remembered in the soul.

At first glance, recent brain research might suggest that soul memories are stored in the brain and therefore, when all is said and done, they are merely the physical preservation of sensory impressions. Without doubt, it is correct that sensory impressions are mapped out inside the brain's structure. By now, the corresponding area of the brain has been identified for almost every sensory category. We know where in the brain the sensory impressions find their matching, singular imprints. Also, the release of hormones following a specific sensory impression is linked to neuronal connections. If a certain situation has led to stress, then a similar situation in the future will lead to stress because a neuronal connection now exists between an approaching sensory impression and a specific release of hormones. However, upon closer examination, it is clear that in spite of the soul's dependence upon physical preconditions, soul memory is not a physical process. It is much more a matter of the soul *utilizing* the existing brain structure *in order to* remember that which a person was previously allowed to forget. Human beings are not forced to remember every impression they had or every action they completed. Many things are lost in the unconscious layers of the human psyche. But if something is followed consciously, meaning that the soul is engaged with the consciousness, it is possible to "resurrect" a memory of something. From this perspective, the human soul remembers only those processes it *wants* to remember — suppression of the memory of traumatic experiences is evidence of this — and to which it had an emotional connection. In other words, the capacity for memory, what is preserved in the soul, is dependent upon the presence of the "I." The soul is not a slave to the memories of all events, but rather, the soul ranges through imprints produced in the brain, and the entire body, in order to allow a memory to rise up.

The memory content of the soul, whether it consists of thoughts or feelings, has nothing to do with the neuronal structure of the brain. One does not feel a synaptic connection or a released hormone; they merely make it possible for the inner soul to create a memory. That is why the soul does not remember the arduous hours spent learning to walk or write, or studying grammar in a foreign language, even though all of these things produced imprints in body and especially the brain.

Thus it can be said that next to the physical "memory of matter" (maintaining and regenerating), there is also maintaining that is purely of a soul nature: the memory of thoughts, feelings and emotions, and actions. This process could be named "the development of new faculties or skills."

Such autonomous, deliberately acquired skills remain preserved; they are completely internalized and last into death and beyond. Research into near-death experiences has shown that it is possible to have memories after one leaves the physical body (Lommel, 2011). Such faculties remain with the individuality and can be tied into the next life. This concept helps further our understanding of cultural development.

Development of the Maintaining Life Process during the First Seven Years

Two things stand out when one examines the faculty for physical maintenance in infants and very young children. First, young children's injuries do not bleed any longer than those of older children; the very young possess a strong wound-healing capacity and relatively soft bones. Blunt force or impact injuries almost never result in broken bones, although there may be frightening-looking bruises and abrasions; a day later much of this has already disappeared. In this case, the maintaining life process almost seems a little over the top. Secondly, infants and young children are enormously dependent upon the care of adults. If it were not for cleaning of wounds, putting ice on bruises, dispensing proper medication and making sure of sufficient warmth, even small injuries could represent great danger. A young child cannot understand about keeping a wound clean and sterile, and has hardly any sense for the proper amount of rest and warmth.

It is clear how very little independence the maintaining life process is able to develop in the physical organism of a young child, even though physical preconditions for healing wounds already exist. Just as with the previously described life processes, here also the life process can develop in a healthy way only with care from the outside.

Every healthy young child is able to breathe, keep body temperature within certain limits, take in nourishment, secrete and eliminate, and preserve and regenerate physical forms and functions. However, none of this can develop in a healthy and harmonious way without adults' loving interest and care. The maintaining life process, just like the other life processes, integrates itself into the physical organism during the first seven years of life and afterward works autonomously, in an individualized manner.

If we once again turn our attention to maintaining in the soul, that is, memory, it is quickly apparent that a young child possesses no power to recall a memory from within, without any outside impulse. The force that makes this possible is still attached to the integration of the maintaining life process in the physical body. At first, memory is possible only as physical memory of matter and not as a faculty of the soul. However, the more this force is released as the child gets older, the more she or he is able to remember from within the self. This is an indication that the anchoring of the maintaining process has been brought to a kind of conclusion, and also indicates school readiness, among other things.

Release of the faculty of memory can be easily observed during the first seven years of life and the beginning of the school years.

Shortly after birth a child can remember nothing. Feeding at a mother's breast is not the memory of a successful act of taking in nourishment, but only the result of the sucking reflex. This is not a learning step resulting from the faculty of memory.

After a few months, a baby already "knows" that when she cries Mother or Father will soon appear. A baby realizes there is a connection between crying and the appearance and attention of an adult. Since the baby has made the association, she will stop crying as soon as footsteps are heard. The ability to connect things together, which is still not actual memory, develops further. But when it comes time for movement and speech development, this ability remains in the inner processes involved in learning to walk and speak, and is in no way conscious.

It already looks very different with a child of kindergarten age, even though a child of that age still cannot independently generate memories. However, memories appear every time a sensory impression reminds a child of something that happened in the past. There is a distinction to be made, however; a child does not remember from out of the self, but rather, the memory of something simply occurs. This is an important distinction. A three- or four-year-old is almost never able to remember something that happened yesterday, even if asked about it. A child simply makes the connection between a sensory impression and something that took place. It may happen that when a child is washing her hands at home she may begin saying a verse or singing a song because that is what was done in kindergarten. Because these things often go hand in hand with completely unnoticed impressions it sometimes looks as though young children can already very well remember things from the past. The fact that a four-year-old can do a finger-game at home or even perfectly recount a whole story that was told in kindergarten always has a connection with a sensory impression: certain hand movements made by a parent, or sitting on a chair like during story time. Such associations will remind the child of the finger game or the story. The memories do not come from within the child; he needs a "marker," an outer form, in order to be able to remember something. It is exactly the same as when people in earlier times literally put up "markers" in the form of memorials and monuments so they could remember events.

Certainly, there are times when very many remembered things will light up in five- and six-year-olds, but they cannot yet rely on their memory. Nevertheless, they continue to practice remembering, especially during the course of the seventh year. During this time period children enjoy being assigned a small task, which they then reliably complete. They now often are able to keep something in mind without falling back into complete forgetfulness with the next impression. In kindergarten it often happens that games from the morning will be taken up again in the afternoon and played in exactly the same way. It also happens fairly often that, while taking off their shoes in the morning, children will begin discussing what they will need to build the exact same house, boat, or airplane as it was done yesterday.

The situation often looks very different with a ten-year-old. She already has all the school subjects and their current topics plus all her homework assignments firmly in her consciousness. Normally, at this age, a child does not need to look in her assignment notebook to know what homework she has. She sits down, thinks about it, and then it comes to her. She can now always remember from out of her own self what she wants to remember.

Since this development is the result of the anchoring of the maintaining life process, it is so important not to ply a preschool-age child with penetrating questions and try to stimulate the memory. If that happens, forces that are still needed for anchoring the life process of maintaining are diverted from the physical body formation process. Only when anchoring is complete does remembering not cause damage to the physical-etheric aspects. Then the maintaining process works autonomously, and the forces present for integration into the physical body become free for soul activities.

When someone is ill, all of the healing, maintaining forces are needed to get healthy again. From self-observation, everyone knows that during illness the ability to remember is dampened. Whenever something in the physical body needs to heal, the maintaining forces for memory are not fully at our disposal.

Growing

Besides the life processes of breathing, warming, nourishing, secreting and maintaining which have already been presented, all living things have processes in their physical organisms that are there "purely" for growth. The lungs, liver, kidneys, other internal organs, nervous system, bones, muscles — in short, every single formation within the human body grows during the course of childhood and youth. At the same time, only in the first few years of life are the forms individualized and changed and their function maintained in accordance with how an individuality has taken hold of the process of growing. In other words, forms and structures established during the first seven years will be increasingly "filled-out" with material over a period of years.

The growing processes proceed rhythmically, resulting in increased height and weight, and are influenced by the stream of heredity, life conditions, and especially by the individuality itself. It is important to keep in mind that growth in the human organism proceeds at varying tempos, which significantly affects behavior because all the functions of life and the senses have to settle back down into a harmonious whole after each period of growth.

The life process of growing requires all the other life processes as pre-conditions. There is no growth without maintained substance, no maintaining without orderly secretions, and so on.

Physical Growth

The body's proportions drastically change during the period of growth. As Bernhard Lievegoed noted in *Phases of Childhood*, a newborn's head comprises fully one-quarter of total body length, while that of an adult comprises only one-seventh to one-eighth of total body length. He also described the following steady changes in height and weight:

Phase: 0 – 1 year - Infancy – Growth in Length
Phase: 2 – 4 years – Toddler – Weight (filling out)
Phase: 5 – 7 years – Preschool – Height
Phase: 8 – 10 years – Elementary School – Weight (filling out)
Phase: 11 – 13 years – Middle School – Height
Phase: After puberty; the third phase of filling out and maturing

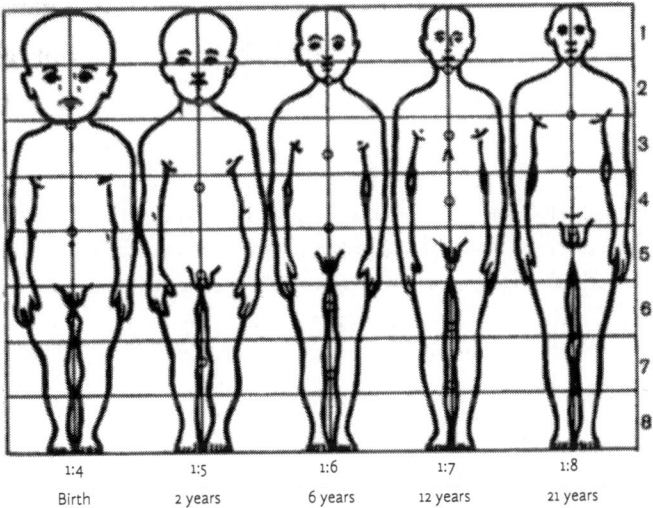

FIGURE 15

Changes in body proportions from infancy to adulthood (head:body ratio).
Source: Lievegoed, 2005

During the first few days after birth an infant loses weight. Just as with all the other life processes, it takes time until this process begins to work in harmony with the others.

Within six months a baby has usually doubled its weight, and has grown about 15 cm (about six inches). At twelve months body weight is triple the birth weight and body length has increased 50 percent since birth.

Compared to animals, human beings have the longest growth period; at the age of fourteen or fifteen humans grow about 6 cm per year (about 2 ½ inches). Girls usually reach their full height between age seventeen and nineteen. This is a little earlier than boys, whose growth period often lasts into their twenty-first year.

During the time of growth one can observe these rhythms of lengthening and filling-out, and such reoccurring rhythms also emerge in the limbs. In embryos the limbs first grow from the periphery. A growth spurt is especially visible in the feet of eleven- or twelve-year-old boys.

But one can get even more detailed in the differentiations. A newborn cannot yet cross its hands over its head, nor even barely touch its hands together, but a preschooler is already able to reach over the head with the right arm and touch the left ear. At birth, the skull is as wide as the torso and the chin still shrunken and small. There is no recognizable neck and the ribs are still horizontal. The little spine is slightly bowed, a delicate C shape. Through the process of learning to stand upright, the spine is brought to its complete, independent form. Much depends on its development since the spine has a massive influence on our later health. The hips are not yet in an upright position. The little legs are only about one-and-a-half times the length of the head, and the feet are turned inward and cannot carry the body. Human beings have to first gain function in the joints. Through healthy, free development of motion the limbs are formed, and through muscle growth they are "aligned." It is fascinating to watch how a child stands upright and moves within space and time as if he has higher knowledge about when to take the next step and when the next phase of development should be undertaken, in harmony with the growth of the body. *Any outside interference at this stage is massively damaging!*

At this point the form of a young child's body is already very different; proportions have shifted, the head appears smaller and the torso and limbs are noticeably longer. The spine of a three-year-old has already changed its form, the ribs become more perpendicular and the hips are upright, with the abdomen protruding slightly. The legs change from being a little bowed to slightly knock-kneed. The knees come forward more and more during the course of development as the feet flatten themselves to the earth.

Up to the seventh year the body stretches; it adds length and, above all, the limbs and joints emerge. The long, hollow bones grow tremendously; likewise for the lower jaw. In the mouth, the permanent teeth, which have long remained hidden in the jaw, now start to become visible.

Sinus cavities have formed in the head and the face becomes more contoured. The neck has grown and the child seems slimmer. There is a recognizable waist since the ribs have reached their permanent form. By the seventh year the S-curve in the spine has formed and the feet are likewise fully formed with the Achilles tendon normally pointing straight down to the earth.

At school age, a child's lanky form begins to fill out and then again more lengthening occurs during the pre-puberty years, beginning with growth in the legs and feet. High-water pants, shoes too small within a few weeks, sleeves too short just at the time one would like to hide the hands; these are all typical occurrences during this time period. Besides all that, children seem to be running into things all the time; the soul is not able to grow along so quickly.

In this phase especially, growth seems to be visible from month to month, but what we cannot see is that the internal organs do not grow in tandem with the outer body. For instance, during this time the heart and lungs are still comparatively small and have to grow to catch up.

With every growth spurt the entire soul structure goes off kilter. All the life processes have to establish new relationships with each other and all the sensory organs have to conquer the new proportions. The child has to master this incredible process with her life energy while, at the same time, often being distracted by intellectual demands from the adult world.

Inside the physical organism, the glands and their functions take on an important role in the growing process, even though they are primarily organs of secretion. They play a role within the metabolic processes, reproduction, and of course growth.

If one examines the glands from the head downward one sees great differences in the functions of the pineal gland, pituitary gland, epithelial glands, thyroid, the thymus gland in front of the heart sac, the adrenal glands, the insulin mechanism in the pancreas, and the sex glands. They all react to changing environmental influences, however; and they are also in a state of interdependency with the soul's behavior. Most of the glands are active from birth; only the sex glands develop their activity in pre-puberty, while the thymus gland begins to degenerate during this time period.

Different hormones (Greek word *hormas* = drive, stimulate) are produced in the glands which contain very specifically formulated substances with either a stimulating or slowing effect on organ activity. In the whole "fluid-being," a term Rudolf Steiner used to describe the bearer of the etheric body, only very small amounts of hormones are found that have external effects. The hormones secreted from the glands combine with protein and are transported by the blood to their destination.

A variety of problems can occur because of under-functioning or over-functioning glands; the best-known are thyroid problems.

The pituitary gland is of central importance. It is positioned in the middle of the head like an observant captain at the wheel of the glandular system. Its activity connects the activity of the nervous system, as a vehicle of perception, with the activity of the metabolic system. The growth hormone, somatotropin, is produced in the acidophilic cells of the pituitary gland; here also the gonadotropin hormone is produced which helps regulate the activity of the sex glands in adults.

If there is under-functioning of the pituitary frontal lobe, then growth disturbances occur (for example, pituitary dwarfism), or problems with the metabolism, mostly fat metabolism, or problems with genitalia.

If there is over-functioning then pituitary gigantism can occur, or secondary growth in protruding body parts such as nose, chin, fingers or toes.

The thyroid gland also affects metabolic processes, and therefore growth. It is located in front of the larynx. It is in a kind of continual conversation with the pituitary gland. "The most important function of the thyroid gland is to produce the hormone thyroxin, which is known for its iodine content" (Faller, 2004). This hormone stimulates growth. Calcitonin, which inhibits bone loss, is also produced in the thyroid gland.

The adrenal glands, which are connected to calcium levels in the blood, help with formation of bone tissue. The thymus gland, which is especially well-developed in newborns, transforms itself into fatty tissue with the onset of puberty. The hormones secreted by the thymus gland inhibit the development of the sexual organs and play a role in growth.

Glands in the testicles (exocrine and endocrine; that is, secretions to the outside and inside), produce sperm cells as well as the male sex hormone, testosterone, which goes directly into the bloodstream and helps with changing the body shape during the growing process.

The ovaries, like the testicles, are also exocrine and endocrine glands. Like all glands, the female sex glands are closely connected to the pituitary gland. Its rhythmic cycle influences the whole living organism. At about ten or eleven years old the female mammary glands start to grow; occurrences in the soul have a special influence on growth at this time.

The connection between growth and glandular functions clearly shows that the growing process, like the processes of maintaining, secreting and reproducing, cannot be seen as separate from the continual production of hormones. During the growth period, new cells are continually produced in the body and transported to the appropriate places. This process is a mysterious wonder that is always trying to live in harmony with the whole while dealing with environmental influences, soul stimuli, and physical events. As a health regulator and basis for the immune system, the glandular system is connected to all the life processes, strongly influences growth, and is intensively tied into the process of reproducing.

However, growth has aspects that are not readily visible. Every organ grows into its specific form. The tiny lung spreads itself out, the stomach grows into its lengthened form, and the liver can grow throughout its existence. The dynamic of the growing process develops differently in every organ, and the activity of every organ spreads throughout the entire body like an effective system of forces. Rudolf Steiner described the effectiveness of this system as being so far-reaching that its activity at locations throughout the body is what allows a material, visible organ to be created and grow in the first place.

According to Steiner in Lecture 5 of *An Occult Physiology* (GA 128), the organs "first exist in the supersensible realm and then, under the influence of the most varied supersensible systems of forces, they are filled with physical material." Within embryonic development one can come to an understanding of these processes if one studies the formation of the heart; first the blood begins to move, to pulse, and then the heart organ, which is not to be understood as a pump, gradually develops.

This thought process can help us to arrive at an understanding of healing. In medicine, there is still the question of how it is possible for a broken bone to heal with hardly a crack visible. The younger the person the more effective the healing power due to the workings of the forces involved in the processes of maintaining and growing.

The system of forces in the etheric body, which Steiner also described as the "master builder" and "architect," allows the physical organism, along with the effects of the soul and spirit, to grow into a form which serves the soul and spirit as a living physical instrument for earthly existence.

Growth of the Soul and Spirit

Just as the physical body grows, the soul does too. Everything involving practice and improvement has to do with soul growth. The connection between physical development and soul development is clear when one considers that playing the piano, for example, is not possible without the fingers first growing flexible enough.

The connection between physical body development and soul development is also recognizable in the physiognomy of early childhood. During the first two to three years, a young child lives within a situation where the primary concern is building up the structure of the nerve-sense system; that is, getting to know the world. So brain development, which goes hand in hand with nerve-sense development, is mirrored externally by a comparatively large forehead. The eyes are situated almost in the middle between the crown of the head and the chin. As for development of faculties, by the end of this developmental phase a child is able to make thought connections and associations. An example: A three-year-old girl runs down the incline from a bridge, again and again, as fast as she can. When the little jaunt is over she hurries back to her room, without taking off her shoes or jacket, places a small board at an incline against the back of a chair. As she sets a little toy car at the top of the board, she says to herself: "It goes faster this way!" The soul grows into the thinking and begins to make natural connections based on a child's own experiences.

During the third to the fifth years, the internal organs are forming more into their individual shapes, the ribs descend and the baby belly disappears. During this time a child is mainly oriented toward imagination-filled internalization of the world. A child more intensely receives the variety of soul-aspects in the world and imaginatively "breathes" them out again with "woof" and "meow" and other role-playing games. The life of this rhythmic system is evident in a child's face when the middle part of the face begins to grow. The forehead is less prominent and the distances between eyes, nose and mouth become greater. Sawdust that falls from a workbench in the kindergarten is urgently needed by some children to feed their horses; other children gather it up and sprinkle it onto imaginary food; for one child it is cheese and for another, powdered sugar. The world is endlessly changeable. The physical instrument is being tuned for the later life of feeling; the soul begins to grow into the feeling nature.

Toward the middle of the first seven years, around age five, the chin and bridge of the nose are more accentuated. This is also the time when the limbs begin to noticeably grow in length. Between ages five and seven, children play more with seesaws and catapults and need a lot of room to move. The world is maneuvered and explored with the limbs. At the same time, children are awakened to ideas and many "plans" are made: "Come on, let's build a seesaw like yesterday. We'll need a board and a block of wood, the same size as yesterday. Mrs. Miller, can we have the big block of wood?" The soul begins to grow into the will nature. By the end of the first seven years the foundation has been laid for the soul faculties of thinking, feeling and willing. This process is mirrored in the changes in a child's face.

Soul faculties and skills grow and expand through constant practice and trying things out. This always happens at an individual's own pace from one's own inner impulses. At this age, implicit learning is the most essential, important form of learning; self-awareness, self-confidence and self-assessment are the results. The "I" is able to comprehensively develop. At the same time, through the development of faculties, the "I" is able to take seeds into a next life; the individuality grows.

Development of the Growing Process during the First Seven Years

One is able to intensively observe the three most important human activities — walking, speaking, thinking — within the first seven years of life: "... one is unable to observe human beings if one cannot tell the difference between their inner and outer nature. When it comes to that which is contained within the whole human being in the form of body, soul and spirit, one has to acquire the ability to recognize subtle differences, if one is going to be dealing with people in a didactic-educational way" (Steiner, *The Child's Changing Consciousness as the Basis of Pedagogical Practice*, GA 306, Lecture 3).

In the act of learning to walk and explore the world of movement, we observe how the child is immersed into the structure and dynamics of the external world, as well as the internal, destiny-laden workings of the individuality. In the act of learning to speak, we observe a gradual mastery of the tools of language, as well as the workings of the soul-body, which also contributes to the development of form. In observing a child learning to think, we are able to recognize more and more the effects of etheric forces that are being released.

These three human activities go through intensive growth processes in the first three years in the form of expansion, improvement, and mastery. By age three, the first stage of each of the three activities is complete: upright motion, speech, and thought. This is the period when the emphasis is on object-based play and games involving the physical body. There is a second stage in play development involving role-playing. A child slips into the mood and atmosphere in the surroundings and transforms his speaking ability, which is stimulated purely through imitation. A two-year-old has a vocabulary of about fifty words, but a three-year-old has already mastered a vocabulary of about two hundred words, with the beginnings of sentence structure and grammar, and has also begun to use the different verb tenses. A five-year-old can hold a conversation in which she uses all her gained abilities and also begins to understand perspective; provided, of course, that language is alive in the surroundings! In the subsequent third stage of play — imaginative play — thinking, feeling and willing are linked, out of a child's own impulse, after he or she has gone through the tedium of boredom. There is completely self-motivated placement of the self into the structure of the world. Walking on stilts, balancing, building high towers: everything invites understanding of the world.

The will for purposeful activity and eagerness to learn about the outside world have awakened, and the faculty that works to build up the physical body is released. This will and these expanding faculties can no more be produced by education than can the faculties of interest and concentration in connection with breathing and warmth production be influenced by education. A child gains these faculties from out of the self, wholly and completely.

Producing – Reproducing

At this point, it is becoming more and more difficult to view a single life process as an isolated process. The glandular functions described in the previous chapter steadily produce hormones. New cells are continually formed in our body and transported to their appropriate destinations. The life process of maintaining brings the newly-formed substances, triggered by the growing process, to the "right" place.

In the following section, we will try to intellectually explore only the life process of *producing*, even though it can never function separately from all the other life processes.

How do we draw closer to this miracle of production?

The human body continually produces the most varied substances:

- *Cells* appear in many different forms, all of which are at the physical organism's disposal for growth and maintenance.
- *Hormones* provide impulses and a driving force throughout the body.
- *Vitamins* are important for maintaining and preserving.
- *Fluids* are streaming carriers of the etheric body, which makes life in and with the world possible in the first place.

All of these things *serve* the etheric body, the architect and master builder, in order for the visible physical body to be recognized as a process that has come to rest. Reproduction means to enable possibility.

Physical Production

The following examples are given in order to put together a picture of the unceasing production processes (see Faller, 2004).

Example – Cell Division: Most of the cells in the body are capable of division. This is what makes growing and maintaining (regeneration) possible in the first place. Every cell, whether it is a skin cell, mucous membrane cell, or a blood cell, consists of several organelles, which are small cell organs that hold together within a cell just like organs in the body. A special component of every cell is the nucleus. It contains chromosomes upon which genetic information is inscribed. After a certain period of time, depending on the type of cell and a person's age, doubling of the nucleus occurs. The x-chromosomes, which can be clearly identified under a microscope, divide their four "arms" lengthwise and four genetically identical chromosome-arms (chromatids) make their way to a corner of the cell nucleus. Next, the nucleus divides itself in the middle and from now on there are two nuclei.

The two nuclei separate from each other, and the parent cell, within which the nuclei are swimming in plasma, also separates itself. Two identical daughter cells have been produced, each holding half of the organelles found in the parent cell. These organelles can now be reproduced, the cells are able to carry out metabolic activity, and the daughter cells can divide again.

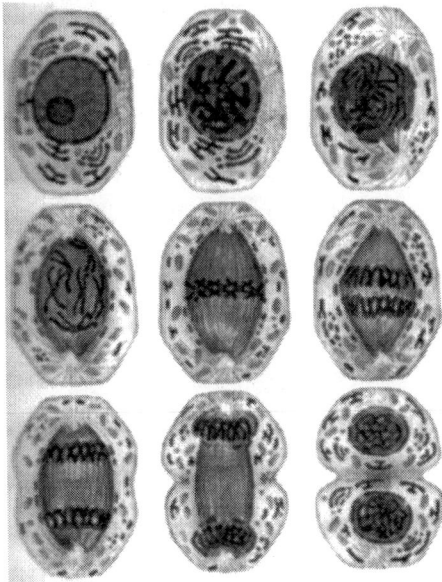

FIGURE 16

Stages of cell division.

Source: http://www.bub-interaktiv.de/ product -info.php/info/p2773_Zellteilung-I– Mitose- - -gro- - -mit-Bestaebung.html

This is a simplified version of the cell division process, which in reality is highly complex and goes through several separate phases. It is subject treated at length in textbooks on biology, physiology and medicine. If we do not wish to lose ourselves in anatomical details, we should just keep in mind that cell division represents an enormously powerful human reproduction process. The lifespan of a healthy skin cell is about four weeks, whereas the average lifespan of a mucous membrane cell in the small intestine is only about one to four days. Accordingly, new cells have to be produced through cell division as often as necessary.

Especially striking is the reproduction of male sperm cells in the testicles (around 85 million per day) and the formation of red blood cells in the bone marrow (around 160 million per minute!).

Example – Blood Formation: Blood formation is a good example of how producing, as a *process*, is spread throughout the physical organism. If one examines the places where blood components are created, then one will notice how the body as a whole is harmoniously attuned. Red blood cells (erythrocytes), white blood cells (leukocytes), and cell platelets (thrombocytes) are produced in the bone marrow. In contrast, the proteins contained in the blood plasma (the colorless, liquid component of blood) are almost all produced in the liver. Among these are blood coagulation proteins, transport proteins, and proteins necessary for the body's immune system. However, the protein molecules in the blood known as antibodies (immunoglobulin) are not produced in the liver. They are produced by a specific class of white blood cells called B-lymphocytes.

Regarding protein production, on several occasions — for example, in the lecture cycles *Illness and Therapy* (GA 313) and *From Sunspots to Strawberries* (GA 354) — Rudolf Steiner brought up the connection between inhaling and exhaling the "spirit-substance" nitrogen and the formation of new protein molecules. This connection is still an open field for research.

Furthermore, blood cells in the unborn are not produced in the bone marrow, but mainly in the liver. Only after birth are blood cells produced exclusively in the bone marrow.

In humans, the lymphatic system in humans, including the thymus gland, spleen, lymph nodes, and tonsils influences blood composition, so we get the image of a blood formation process that is absolutely not limited to a specific location, but rather is spread throughout the body as a production process.

Example – Hormone Production: The endocrine system is a further example of the body's unceasing production process. Many endocrine hormone glands produce the most varied signaling substances, which are divided among lymph or blood vessels and are driving forces in the body.

Hormones are messengers (not cells, but molecules) that influence metabolic processes in the cells.

The most familiar hormones and their locations are: adrenaline in the adrenal glands; insulin and glucagon in the pancreas; estrogen in the ovaries; androgen in the testicles.

One can clearly see that hormone production is also spread throughout the body. Besides the locations named above, the following should also be mentioned: The pituitary gland, the pineal gland, the placenta, the nervous system (with formation of neurotransmitters), and the liver and kidneys.

The body produces impulse-giving, driving substances continuously in many different places so that the body "functions" as an instrument of the soul. With certain illnesses involving hormone secretion, the task of hormones to provide physical impulses and possibilities becomes especially apparent; for example, depression goes hand in hand with hormonal imbalance.

Example – Human Reproduction: Naturally, human reproduction occupies a special place within the realm of producing. The formation of sperm cells and egg cells, and the formation of a new human body through the merging of the two during the act of procreation, represent the most significant phenomenon of production within the human organism.

The first special aspect is the polarity of male sperm cells and female egg cells. There are around 85 million mobile sperm cells produced in the male testicles daily and they are among the smallest cells in the human body. In contrast, only one immobile egg cell per month (rarely two) matures in the female uterus. This is the largest cell in the human body. All the egg cells that mature over a woman's lifetime are already present in her ovaries when she is born. Within every monthly cycle a new uterine lining is produced.

The second special aspect is the merging of a sperm cell and an egg cell. The first part of this process is a chaotic and unpredictable merging together of two hereditary lineages which then leads to development of an embryo.

We are not going to go into detail about the stages of embryo development. However, relative to the producing – reproducing life process, it is of decisive importance that the endless possibilities for characteristics of future offspring are already established during the formation of the genitals and reproductive cells. Earlier we said that the producing – reproducing process serves the etheric body, the architect, as it works to make visible a process which has come to rest, represented by the physical body. The expression "reproduction means to enable possibility" is immediately apparent in offspring created by the processes of procreation and reproduction. Almost nothing is predetermined for the developing human being inside a mother's womb. Almost everything is open! The moment of chaos when the egg and sperm cells merge is the most visible expression of reproducing as possibility, not as predetermination. This is easily observed in families with several children, who show their differences not only as the result of growing and developing under the influence of different environments, but from day one. Every woman who has had more than one child knows that the differences between children are noticeable already during pregnancy.

Material Substance, Genetics and Epigenetics

Examining aspects of reproduction, whether of individual parts of the physical body, production of forms and functions, or reproduction of a complete physical organism, leads to some questions: What exactly is human material substance? How is the formation of single molecules or cells connected to the etheric body, the builder of the physical body, and the individuality that lives within it?

The word "substance" is rooted in the Latin word "substantia," which means "a holding or an asset," "being or existence," or "embodiment." The verb "substare" means "to be present within something." In the German language, even today, the word "substance" can also mean "the presence of a framework or infrastructure" or "a fixed supply," besides the more familiar meaning of "material" or "matter." Examination of the derivation of the word "substance" helps us gain a deeper understanding of the (re)producing processes in human beings. If human material substance appears to be all-inclusive — that is, if the "being" part of a human being appears to exist in human material substance — then it stands to reason that the "being" is also present in the physical manifestation of the human body. This means that the forms and functions of the human body are not random, but are the physical expression of the essence, the "being" aspect, of a human being. Essentially, the physical form of a human being has more to do with the "being" aspect than with physical matter. From this perspective, the phrase, "reproduction means to enable possibility," becomes even more significant.

The reproducing process brings forth germ cells that merge together during fertilization to form a completely new substance that has never been in the world before. From out of a new totality, that is, the dividing stem cells, single cell types are differentiated. At the beginning of embryonic development the endoderm, ectoderm, and embryonic disc are differentiated. In later development, the differentiation process forms the organs, limbs, and so forth. The possibility of a child "coming into being" is already present in the reproductive capacities of the mother and father. More specifically, it is the possibility of a child coming into being as a potentiality which, after being created by the individuality, is grasped by the physical aspect and made available to a child's etheric body as a model. At the same time, it can be seen that the characteristic of a "totality" of germ cells, from out of which it is still possible for everything to come into being, gradually disappears during the course of the differentiation process. In the first few days after fertilization, the dividing stem cells are not specific regarding the types of cells that may come into being — everything is still possible: ear, hand, or foot. As the differentiation process progresses, individual cell types are increasingly limited in their possibilities. Later on, a hair cell cannot be used to form a kidney, even though they have both developed from one and the same fertilized egg cell. During the course of fetal development, the closer spirit approaches to matter, the more the inherited material is differentiated according to the intentions of the etheric body. At birth, it is not only the physical forms that are born, but also the functions; that is, breathing, warming, nourishing and so on also come into the world.

So, the circle is complete. The reproduction processes of the parents are able to bring forth the seven life processes of the child.

When we consider the physical body model inherited from parents it immediately becomes apparent that a child's individuality is not slavishly bound to the inherited body. The physical model is comparable to the raw material an artist uses to create a sculpture. Initially, almost every possibility is present within the substance of inherited raw material, just as almost any form can be sculpted from a block of wood. The individualized imprint of the etheric body, as architect and master builder, is evident in the differentiation.

Since environment also plays an important role in transforming the inherited body, it should be noted that the individuality, heredity, and social milieu all work together when it comes to forms, functions, characteristics, and faculties of human beings.

Epigenetic research clearly shows that, in gaining a physical body of one's own, the parents' genes are a prerequisite in the beginning, but they are not the determining factors (Blech, 2010). In the meantime, the idea of predetermination by the parents' genes has been conclusively disproven by science. Today, science tells us that certain genes are activated and others are deactivated, according to whether or not protein building blocks found around naked DNA allow the expression of a genetic code or block it. One no longer speaks only of the human genome, but also the epigenome. The human epigenome is subject to constant change! There have even been many studies done which verify the existence of epigenetic heredity. That means that the parents' lifestyle plays a role in blocking certain genes, not allowing them to come to expression, in their children and even their grandchildren. In connection with this idea, Rudolf Steiner formulated the main rule of education: "The educator's own etheric body has to be able to affect the physical body of a child; and this has to happen as a result of teacher training" (*Education for Special Needs*, GA 317, Lecture 2).

Understanding the gene as a kind of basic prerequisite which is always very alterable, and remains so, shows the possibility of a self-acquired physical body, permeated with individuality, which even has consequences for future generations. Spirit permeates matter and brings it forth as something new, but spirit is not determined by matter.

Production in the Soul and Spirit

First and foremost, production in the soul requires a certain harmony of soul in order to be able to properly produce an action, feeling, or thought. Production of antibodies against pathogens, healthy hormone levels, creating a healthy balance in the body (homeostasis), and, of course, the healthy development of individual body organs, are all prerequisites for soul harmony, which consequently allows for the possibility of producing something in the soul at all levels. When all is said and done, a human action is a process of production in the soul: "I want to go for a walk now, and I will do it." This is brought forth from the soul; perhaps not as a free decision, but maybe because of some internal or external compulsion. Nevertheless, it does come from the soul. A feeling is also brought forth from the soul. In most cases it does not happen in freedom, but it is brought forth in any case. Soul production is especially visible in the area where freedom normally prevails; namely, in the realm of ideas. Wherever the thought life of a human soul turns to creating something new is where ideas are brought forth, which the individuality may even turn into ideals. The creative power of the soul to produce ideas is a primal human characteristic that differentiates us from animals more decisively than any of the other soul faculties. It leads to the formation of ideals, artistic activities, discoveries, and true knowledge. Soul production is therefore of the utmost importance when some real knowledge, perception, or awareness is on hand that needs to remain with the individuality. After perceiving some specific thing, according to interest and inner connection, in the end, one's own creative, inner capacity for reproduction has to be engaged, otherwise there is no realization, recognition, or understanding of the perception. I do not understand anything about a table until I use all my senses to perceive it with interest and then recreate it within myself. I have to once produce the concept of a table before I can recognize it again. The faculty of being able to grasp a concept, to *create*, is first released over the course of childhood.

An abstract thought is also not truly understood until it has been creatively (re)produced within the self. Interest, analysis, questioning, and even regular interaction with a thought, are still not enough to achieve real understanding. I have to be able to develop the thought myself, out of my soul, before it is truly grasped. If, initially, they are thoughts with which the individuality has united itself and which work as outside entities to produce the forms and functions of our physical being, then, over the course of childhood, there is an increasing ability to create and understand ideas, concepts, and thoughts. A child who is ready for school clearly exhibits how idea formation, recalling memories, and understanding thoughts all have to do with the birth of the etheric body. From now on, the etheric body with its seven life processes is no longer mainly occupied with transforming the inherited physical body, but rather frees itself more and more from that exclusive task. The ability to create thought pictures, which is noticeably in the foreground of school-readiness, shows that *human beings think with the etheric body; that is, with the processes of the etheric body and the organ-forming forces that are freeing themselves from being exclusively bound to the physical body.* The released thought forces are now available to the soul as one of its faculties.

Active movement between things of the world and active composition and prioritizing of perceptions in order to assign them meaning also belong in the category of soul production, which is slowly established over the course of childhood. It is my released production forces that understand, discover, or create a concept or idea. Human beings are permanent creators of their own selves and the world.

The will to identify or discern something may also be counted among things that are produced in the spirit, for which self-acting soul or spirit organs of perception are developed. We are not only referring to the development of certain supersensible organs of perception on the path to higher knowledge, but also the active intention to develop the capacity to perceive things for which no "natural" organs of perception exist. All parents and educators know how one cannot avoid developing a sense for what a child is really trying to say, even though he is unable to adequately express it. Outer circumstances initiate an especially strong impulse to develop these organs of perception at certain times: "the terrible twos" before a child learns to talk, the crisis at the beginning of the change of teeth, the "Rubicon" around age nine or ten, and during puberty, for example. Parents, caregivers, and teachers have to search for understanding of the being standing before them and develop appropriate organs of perception for each and every child. It may happen that formerly reliable concepts seem not to "fit" a certain child, or are not applicable in this case. New ways of understanding have to be found. This is an example of a creative act of spirit.

Integration of the Producing Process during the First Seven Years and Its Transformation

Producing of individual, physical forms and functions stands in the foreground of the entire developmental phase up to school-age. The physical body inherited from the parents has to be transformed according to the requirements of a child's individuality and made his own. A child has to gradually "produce" his own body, which includes the outer form, dexterity of the limbs, speech, flexibility in the life of ideas, concepts, and imagination, and especially the function of each individual sensory organ, as well as the internal organs. Eyes and ears, stomach and intestines — everything has to first learn its purpose. Therefore, the task of education in the first seven years is to create an enveloping, protective, and stimulating environment for the production of individual forms and functions.

In this respect, that which a young child produces at first is very closely connected with the environment. At the beginning of "the terrible twos," with the descent of the ribs, and, around age three, when the hips move to an upright position: this is the time when a child begins to have a sense of her own condition or state. A certain sensitivity emerges, whereas before often only purely vegetative expressions occurred, such as crying when hungry or tired. The way a young child cries, moves, stands upright, and learns to talk is always different with each individual. In spite of this, the soul aspect of these expressions remains, like a mirror of the environment; that is, a mirror of the individual, physical life processes.

During play, it is usually only after age three that the activity of imagination is unleashed. Before this time there was "only" object-based play, which had more to do with sensory experiences than with taking things of the world into the soul and bringing them out again. If, however, this all progresses in the proper order, then around age five more thoughts and ideas begin to emerge; this thing or the other simply must proceed in a certain way, and play will also follow along with more and more awakening ideas. Nevertheless, it must be clearly stated that young children almost never have an "original" idea for play, as remarkable as that sounds. If one closely observes kindergarten children at play (even the "big" six-year-olds), one finds that the impulses for play are almost always found in the circumstances and experiences of the outside world, and sometimes also in internal bodily processes — an example would be destroying things when digestive activity is too strong. One will hardly ever see a completely original idea!

That which is brought to the outside, produced and reproduced, is heavily dependent on the three stages of physical development in the first seven years, as can be seen from the following descriptions.

From birth to the first appearance of the "I"-consciousness and the "terrible twos" phase around age two-and-a-half, the nerve-sense system is transformed and most of the neuronal network for a person's entire life is established at this time. The vegetative, body-bound expressions and object-based play described above predominate.

Up to the fifth year, the rhythmic system is transformed, the ribs descend, lungs grow larger and breathing is deeper. Imaginative activities which are drawn from experience predominate during play.

After age five, producing more ideas is made possible by continued lengthening of the body and the head being raised above the body because of a longer neck. Simultaneously, the body's metabolic-limb system is being individualized. This results in play in which ideas are brought together with the possibilities offered by the surrounding space, materials, and one's own body. Play is now repeated over and over again, and even continued the next day, with an understanding of the space in which it occurs.

Just as play behavior has been showcased here, the development of language can be examined in the same way. The possibilities of producing language are also dependent upon physical production. Only by experimenting with speech sounds, as well as having examples of speaking and singing in the surroundings, is it possible to form words out of babble with the gradual development of the larynx. Furthermore, after the second year, the ability to make thought associations and connections depends upon the release of etheric forces resulting from the production of neuronal structures.

Looking beyond the first seven years, it is clear that the first opportunity of forming ideals and wider social concepts, or even utopian ideas, occurs with the formation of the sexual organs (and the simultaneous degradation of the thymus gland). As it goes along with the maturation of the possibility of procreation, the producing process is the slowest of the seven life processes when it comes to detaching from the physical aspect of a human being.

From this perspective, it appears that the release of the soul faculties of thinking, experience of feelings, and development of practical life skills at the beginning of school-age is like having reached one level on the way to the release of the producing processes. The transformation of the producing process into soul faculties comes to its tentative conclusion through the renewed filling-out of the physical body around the tenth year (Rubicon), followed by the emergence of stronger feelings that accompanies the body lengthening and sexual maturity that occurs around the twelfth or thirteenth year (beginning of puberty), with the subsequent formation of concepts, ideas and ideals.

The producing process shows us to what great extent physical formation, the production of forms and functions, is the basic prerequisite for the release of soul faculties. There would be no imaginative play in kindergarten without the bringing forth of interior spaces through growth in the torso; no deepened experience of the "I" during the Rubicon period without renewed filling out of the physical body and a new ratio of breath to pulse (1:4); and no development of completely individual ideas without maturing of the sexual organs. Puberty indicates that a person has reached "Earth-maturity," and, because of released soul-possibilities, is now able to form ideas from out of the self that will be a force in the world.

Once again, it is very clear that if adults address a child too intellectually or force adult concepts on a child too soon, it is a great obstruction to developing the part of self that is totally unique and individual. When that which has been physically produced does not properly disengage, allowing the child's own, unique soul-spirit capacities to rise up, and, instead, a child's capacity for imitation and conformity is misused in order to integrate the child into society, then yesterday's educational notions will act to bring forth the new individual, supplanting the activity of the "I" like a drug. Ideas and feelings about the world and self-motivated actions in the world should be allowed to unfold freely. Allowing for this to happen in a protected environment, without indoctrination, is the task of education. It has to do with providing an environment where children are able to self-develop.

The seven life processes have now all been presented. As mentioned in the chapter on secreting, some processes serve the act of taking in the world and some serve to integrate new things into the world.

Breathing, warming, and nourishing are required in order for human beings to take in something from the world. This is how the world is able to affect human beings.

Maintaining, growing, and reproducing are prerequisites for the ability to give something new to the world; even to the point of a new human body through the act of procreation. This is how human beings are able to affect the world.

The secreting process, with its activities of ordering, sorting, questioning, and analyzing, stands exactly in the middle. This is where the human being encounters itself, in the sleeping unconscious of the physical body, the dreaming half-consciousness of the soul, and in the full consciousness of the spirit. It is significant that Rudolf Steiner spent so much time telling us about the secreting processes (see the section on "Physical Secretion"). We are touching upon things here of the most personal nature: namely, one's own, unique intentions, motives, questions, and judgments, out of which, by way of maintaining, growing, and reproducing, the world is again given something newly created.

Play and Physical Organ Development

Within each individual's biography, his or her very personal, unique motives and questions are the most directly discernible during times of free play as a child. However, free play appears to be threatened with extinction; time and space for free play is disappearing worldwide. We are doing too little to protect a child's right to play, perhaps because we still do not understand it.

Play, one of the most enduring features of childhood, is being squeezed out of existence by a whole array of factors. In play, we find the human ability to develop our life processes at our own pace and intensity. During free play it is amazing to observe with what perseverance, concentration, and inner attentiveness a child bonds with the world, its natural laws and inhabitants. Within play, a child explores and marvels and self-develops.

Rudolf Steiner pointed out that this development is at first mainly physical development. The connection between body-play and body-development, with its significance for the processes of standing upright and overcoming reflexes, up to and including physical formation of the brain, has been extensively researched. The same is true of research into skeletal formation, posture deformities, and the most delicate synaptic connections playing a role in learning difficulties. The brain is not the only thing that is formed within the first few years of life. As has already been explained, the entire inherited body has to be individualized and grasped completely, clear down to the finest structure. A child has to *play*, not learn, so that she can develop unhurriedly and with ease. Children "develop" play from out of their own selves; play works from the inside out. When children are given ample opportunity to explore this new, individual world of the physical body, they are able to seize the world around him with the greatest attentiveness; object-based play develops.

In the following we will attempt to understand, in a rather more pictorial way and perhaps with some repetition, the role of our organs in the development of play. Exploring these physiological aspects may encourage some people to do further research into the subject on their own. Our efforts here involve an attempt to understand respective organs and their gestures of movement in order to formulate thoughts about how particular gestures in an organ can be connected with the gestures of movement in the soul. Rudolf Steiner provided many indications of this connection, in which he explained that in the first years of life the physical body is formed into an instrument for later life. In our attempt at understanding, one basic question that arises is whether or not play mirrors the internal gestures of the organs. Are we able to gain an idea of the formative forces at work by observing play? Furthermore, lest we lose sight of the possible far-reaching consequences, what happens along the path of an individuality's incarnation if free play continues its decline? If we really take seriously the power of imitation in childhood, then we have to take a closer look at the formative forces present in children's surroundings, which serve as a model for their development.

In the embryo the development of organs proceeds from top to bottom, in order to integrate them into the dimensions of space. The seven life processes work in all the organs to varying degrees. The way we personally (*personare* = to sound throughout) play our bodily instrument (tone = sound or muscle tone) largely depends upon our breathing. Our spirit-soul takes hold of and thoroughly breathes into the body and, in this way, forms its physical abode.

Meanwhile, the *brain* has undergone intensive research, even though there are still many questions remaining about its activities. The gesture of the brain is one of receiving and preserving. At the beginning of life these brain activities are intensely experienced during body-play, exploring the physical body until a child is able to formulate the concept: Everything is mine! At this age, it is important not to deter a child from this understanding by subjecting him to cognitive learning. A child is an open, perceiving being and lives very strongly in imitation. That is why it makes more sense to create children's surroundings so that they are able to experience the activities of receiving and preserving, especially during free play. In this way a child will change her behavior completely from out of her own self, when she is internally ready.

Through the sense of touch, the barrier of the physical body is increasingly perceived to be the threshold of the world and, in the active process of standing upright, the *lungs* develop as the organ of interior breathing. The lungs form a vast interior network of branch-like bronchi which have something like tiny spheres at their ends. The walls of the alveoli have to be firm and stable so that their interior space, or cavity, creates a kind of "abode." This can also be seen in the forming of the frontal, paranasal, and maxillary sinus cavities when a child is ready to start school. This tightly enclosed interior space is the basis upon which contour and structure is brought in, even thought structure. Anyone who has ever had an infection in one of these areas has experienced this. However, these cavities should also not become sclerotic, with solidifying forces setting in too early.

With the formation of these physical "walls," there appears in the consciousness a kind of "separation" as well. A harmonious recognition of "you" and "I" can occur through breathing as an experience of the external barrier. "In the case of forced thoughts and actions, the soul aspect of lung activity may become pathological in its effect (anorexia, for example)" (Holzapfel, 2014). Often, by studying pathology, one comes to a better knowledge of organ activity.

Rooms that are always consistent in their arrangement give children the order they need for organ development, because their "being" is still dispersed in the surroundings. This allows children to fully breathe, with complete trust, until they lift themselves out of Earth's heaviness, until they are able to "breathe" far enough down that the foot arches are formed.

Such interior spaces are very intently "played through." With the greatest concentration, a child will fill something and empty it again, over and over, in order to independently conquer the interior spaces in a joyful way and experience the barriers (Peter Rosegger called this activity "breathful play"). How the interior spaces are "played through" varies greatly with each child. It can be observed that with some children the arranging of interior spaces is a big part of their activities; no closet or drawer remains tidy, everything has to be explored. All along the way, such children may find it difficult to settle into calm, deep breathing. For hours they will fill a basket with chestnuts and empty it out again, hide under a table, make a tent using cloth squares, burrow in the sand, roll around on the lawn and touch everything; until the time comes when a child's drawing of a house shows someone peeking out of the window! This is the expression of the child having "come down to Earth." Play is the process of locating oneself on Earth.

The act of "breathing-through," rhythmically taking in and letting go, is very closely connected to the experience of time. This becomes apparent when the position of the hips changes in the third year, the spine becomes straighter and breathing deeper, and the child understands "tomorrow," "today," and "yesterday." Here begins the phase of "the terrible twos."

Many aspects of sensory perception can be included here, since breathing and perception are very closely related. The development lasts until the breathing has matured. The soul's relationship to the physical organs becomes increasingly more apparent. Stress, agitation, lack of rhythm in daily life, adult insecurity that results in the creation of dogmas, and many other things are co-participants in physical formation which, simultaneously, cause the activity of play to ebb away. The organ becomes condensed experience; that is to say, condensed soul life, upon which the soul aspect is mirrored at a later time. Steiner described this in one of a series of essays from *Das Goetheanum* (collected in GA 36):

> First, the soul works on the physical body so that, afterwards, it can be revealed within a free intellect. The development of the soul begins already with thinking itself; which, in turn, is a result of sensory perception. If an object is perceived the soul becomes active. It forms the corresponding body part in such a way that it will be able to develop a mirror image of an object in thoughts. In experiencing this mirror image, the soul is looking at the results of its own activity.

Who is it that guides a child into playing through this process that leads inside and outside, sometimes with more intensity and sometimes with less?

When we consider the emerging human being, we first see that a rhythmically pulsing *bloodstream* is created outside of the embryo. From out of this liquid stream, which grows to the inside, the *heart* is formed. The mover of the crossways-striated (striped) cardiac muscle (which actually is a "voluntary" muscle) is the blood, and the impulse for the movement clearly lies in the spirit-soul realm. We know this phenomenon very well through our waking self-awareness, since blood and heart activity immediately respond to our soul moods and our strong impulses of will.

With the first breath, drawing in the spirit-soul element, the embryonic circulation is closed off and this closure produces a clear separation; arterial and venous blood stand in opposition, as it were. Blood carries our "persona" throughout the body and is in constant motion. It mirrors the condition of our soul. It becomes slower, more viscous, thicker, faster, more active, livelier, or thinner, all according to whether we stand more in the deconstructive nerve-sense-system functions or the constructive metabolic-limb-system functions. Every organ has a finely-tuned regulation process for its changing needs of blood supply (Koob, 2005).

The width of blood vessels is adjusted according to blood flow. In the first years of life it is determined by the organ receiving the blood. All the organs cooperating together are what develop the arterial and venous blood vessel systems.

The soul conditions of the people in a child's surroundings have a very strong influence on this development: how one speaks to a child and, especially, one's behavior toward the child, as well as whether people in a child's surroundings carry out actions that are sensible and well-ordered. These impressions become "imprints" in the physical organism, in a child's heart, and often only reappear in midlife. The blood carries all these impressions to the periphery of the body and back again to the center. The impressions are internalized. We can see the wisdom of the expression "learn by heart." When we perceive something with concentration, and have warmed ourselves for that which we perceive, then the blood gets moving up to the brain. Only when this warmth production is activated can we bring something into our consciousness. However, this also requires rest periods and time. So it is with the course of our lives: a rhythmic pulse consisting of activity and rest enables our heart to come along and we can be completely present with our "I."

The active alternation between being and resting is found to an intense degree in body play and the development of physical motion. If a child, left to his own devices, is allowed to playfully move, he will change his position about every ninety seconds and quietly "listen" to the movement. During the rest periods is when movement is able to become the body, to build the physical body. If we constantly immobilize young children we are hindering this development!

During diaper changes, an infant will beam with joy while playing peek-a-boo with a cloth: "Where are you? There you are!" The separation between "me" and "you" is thoroughly savored and usually accompanied by enthusiastic air-pedaling of little legs. We will most likely grow tired of the game long before the child does. The same is true of the game "Who can run into my arms?" in which the child strolls along the periphery of a circle before shouting and running, completely immersed in the movement, back to the center into waiting arms. The child experiences an arrival, a coming to one's own self and knowing that she is heartily welcomed as "I."

Now let us turn to the function of the kidneys and the "kidney process" during play. During the embryonic period the precursors to the kidneys begin developing in the area of the throat. They travel far down below and then back up again to the area of their permanent placement. Lungs and kidneys are both strongly connected with breathing; the lungs with the living element of oxygen and the kidneys with the light/air element of nitrogen. The kidneys regulate the air element and eliminate fluids. They secrete, sort, differentiate and critically' "question" the substances that end-lessly flow through them (150 to 180 liters filtered daily). Only one to one-and-a-half liters are eliminated per day. The body cavity formation spoken of previously takes place here also, in the renal corpuscle, renal pelvis, and the bladder.

If we compare a newborn infant's kidneys to those of an adult, it becomes clear that the lobule structure has to expand, but first the kidney walls have to develop and become solid to provide a barrier. The sensitive kidneys have an immediate alarm reaction to fear, stress, pressure, etc. Walter Holtzapfel determined: "Every aggravation stops the flow of blood in the kidneys" (Holtzapfel, 2014). This quickly leads to exhaustion and, in time, to illness that may manifest years later.

An inundation of sensory impressions and a hectic pace leave their mark on the kidneys, with the worst of all being trauma in early childhood that blots out the colorfulness of the world. Every impression leaves an imprint!

In children's play we find not only copious amounts of enclosing and "wall-building," but also other activities that correspond with the activities of the kidneys, the completion of which helps the kidneys to develop. When a child develops the "pinch-grip" (at around nine months) and hand-eye coordination has progressed far enough, then the little one discovers every bit of lint, fluff and fuzz. With the first "gesture of antipathy" (palms turned outward) the child begins to recognize the smallest, finest things. Later on a child will eagerly sort and put similar things together. For people with autism, this process remains static, externally and internally. With con-stant repetitions, the autistic person is actually trying to "develop himself out of it" (an actual statement from someone with autism). For healthily developing children, play may also be seen as a process of always-improv-ing digestion, of sorting and differentiating. This process shows itself in a young child's eager questioning, for which no explanatory answers are expected; the child is using questioning as a way of practicing distancing himself. This process is also visible when children are eating, especially only children; they eat with great attentiveness or carefully separate each food on the plate.

This "kidney process" was very clearly visible during play in one of the children in our kindergarten. Almost compulsively, the child constantly watched over the play store; while eating muesli, the oatmeal had to sit next to the sorted fruit with a glass of milk next to it. With hands in pockets, this child watched over the others playing and made comments and questioned their play. The little observer was the birthday cake baker's helper for over a year and on painting days he washed the watercolor glasses so that the most beautiful "temporary pictures" were created in the dishpan (along with many other activities). Gradually, the connecting aspect, the flowing, was so internalized in this child that he was able to tentatively try out new forms of play and perhaps leave the sorting to his kidneys. (This boy is now an adult with a Ph.D. in chemistry!)

Function of the stomach and intestines: One could almost say that the external world "falls through" us by way of the long path through the digestive tract, and we can tell from it how to form our physical substance. We kill substances and then recreate and enliven them in a different form. Through saliva, gastric acid, etc. the substances are split apart and we defend ourselves against them. Johannes Rohen wrote about it: "Instead of two layers of muscle, the stomach has three… It serves as a reservoir that is able to stretch and grow larger without instigating the actual peristaltic action of the intestines" (Rohen, 2007).

In the second segment of the stomach is where "conveyance" first takes place. The larger first segment is only for taking in substances; it holds. Keeping in mind that tensing and relaxing of our muscles is strongly associated with inhaling and exhaling gives one a rudimentary understanding of the formation of the most varied stomach structures. How quickly we get indigestion or how difficult it is to get our digestion going is certainly later very strongly connected with our physicality, with what we were able to build in the first few years of life. Food is broken down into its basic components in the small intestine and is further processed, moved, and split apart so that the fascinating metabolic process in the intestinal wall can be completed. We take in information (*informare* = to bring into form) from the external world in order to form our own substance out of it, to build our own form.

Investigating, tasting, salivating, and deconstructing things down to their smallest parts takes up a large portion of children's play. A taste for the world is awakened more and more. (The many different kinds of tasting a child attempts should not be hindered by her always having a pacifier in her mouth.) Very gradually, but completely from the child's own self, the insatiable desire of "everything is mine" turns into the ability to wait. The result of tasting, along with increased capability of movement, results in the child wanting to "move stuff"; a chair is pushed across the room over and over again and a wooden block is carried from here to there, all seemingly senseless activities in our eyes. The more the soul internally experiences and fills the body as its house, the more intensely it is able to digest the impressions of the world. This maturing process of the digestive tract lasts until Earth-maturity (puberty).

It is difficult to give a short description of the fundamental aspects of the liver, gallbladder, and spleen so that one gets a helpful picture of these organs. It is especially difficult with the liver.

The liver occupies a comparatively large amount of space in an embryo; one could also name this organ the "en-livener" as in enlivening. This "oven" which warms us, or rather, lights us, takes on a dominant role in metabolism. Enlivening processes go on all the time in the liver. Old blood cells destroyed by the spleen are transformed into bile and cells destroyed by light in the retina are transported to the liver and reinvigorated there, and much, much more. The liver must always remain adaptable, yet stable, in all its activities. In this "laboratory" or substance transformation center, there are constant decisions to be made about what happens to the substances, where they are transported, how much should be taken from sugar storage, and so on. If a part of the liver is surgically removed it grows back again. The most exact differentiations and decisions occur in the liver so that every organ is sent "its particular cells." As with all the other organs, the liver process is spread throughout the body, from the sense of taste, which already activates the liver, to the sugar metabolism in the muscles, for example. The liver's gesture of movement is a constant alternation from the outside to the inside and back to the outside again; an enduring "conversation" between the processes of decomposition and formation.

Transformation and enlivening form the most intensive processes in children's play. As long as young children live rather more on the periphery and their body's warmth production still extends beyond the physical sheath, the whole of the surroundings lives with them; they are one with the enlivened world. The more a child fixes her gaze on something specific, comprehends the object, and grasps the dead concept, the sooner she will connect with the hardening decomposition process. If a child is able to play in a lively environment that is open to transformation, development of the liver process is active and adaptable. As has already been mentioned, the liver produces bile from destroyed blood cells. The thickened bile waits in the gallbladder until it is needed for digestion. Bile possesses an aggressive, destructive power. In normal language usage, the word "aggressive" means to go after something too strongly. It is pent-up will-forces. But our physical organism needs this sharp conflict in order to stay healthy. Anger dams up the flow of bile, until it overflows: "If you did not have bile you would become terribly phlegmatic; hands, arms and head would all be hanging down... Human beings must have bile. It has to come from the liver. If the liver is relatively small the person is phlegmatic. If the liver is relatively large the person has a lot of fire within because bile produces fire" (Steiner, GA 351).

A young child is a constant mover. When the will is awake, a child is always trying to explore his physical body and the world and also trying to gradually give his will a purpose. What are we doing to children, these beings of will, when we strap them into seats for hours at a time, unable to move around and at the mercy of the deconstructive processes of the nerve-sense system? Initiative, enthusiasm, and enlivening ideas have hardly any physical basis if a young child has no space to move around and cannot act out and experience free play during childhood.

The way children create a space during play is the same way the spleen creates a space in the body. This organ "creates space" for something new inside the body. During the embryonic stage the spleen is still a "blood producer," but after birth it is a "blood consumer." It acts as a stronghold against invading foreign bodies. Old blood cells are destroyed and transported to the liver, as has been said. Destruction of the old makes way for creation of the new; space for something new is created. For example, destruction is a precondition for individualizing and creating one's own substances out of food substances. As long as a child is breastfeeding this activity in the organism is hardly required. When an infant has a stronger experience of its physical boundary and meets us with his gaze, then begins the slow process of defining and establishing boundaries accompanied by the development of his own immune system.

If we lose the sense of our physical boundary it literally drives us crazy and the destructive will is turned toward the self. This is well known in psychiatry and it has also been seen in experiments with astronauts. The German word "spleen" actually denotes "a crazy idea or whimsical notion."

Who has not seen this kind of enthusiastic play and the joyful look in a child's eyes that accompanies it: A tower is built, and knocked down, over and over; sand pies are baked and arranged in a nice row and — swoop — all are happily destroyed. A child's endurance for such play activities is likely much greater than ours. Let them have this joyfully experienced process and the fire in their eyes!

In adults who are not properly incarnated, as seen with psychiatric illnesses or developmental disabilities, for example, one can clearly see the connections between the organs and the conditions of the soul. With the incarnation process in a young child, such connections can only be dimly sensed. In his *Education for Special Needs* (GA 317) Rudolf Steiner explained: "... the more subtle illnesses ... lie in the fluids coursing through the organs; the liver, for example. Illness lies in the movement of fluids, and even in the movement of gaseous substances coursing through the liver. Thorough warming of such an organ is of very special importance for the life of the soul."

Steiner pointed out that in the case of a young child who exhibits a weak will, one should first ascertain which organ is connected to the weakness so that one's attention can first be directed to organ activity to better understand the child whenever so-called "abnormal behavior" crops up.

When one observes a child's free play during the first few years, can one say that it is primarily a mirror of organ activity and that what is formed internally is externally visible, or that the visible aspect helps to form something internally? Many questions arise, especially when one realizes that the same play impulses are found in all our little Earth citizens, and likewise, their drawings and paintings are images of their body-forming processes.

We have undertaken a rudimentary examination of the importance of play in childhood, as well as the importance of an enlivened environment for organ development as a basis for soul-spirit processes. We have taken a very condensed look at organ development, combined with observations of children's play, and attempted to make the connection between the two. The task of researching this aspect of play is still in the very beginning stages. There should be further observations made and the parameters widened for more research into what we have only touched upon here. The goal is for children to have the possibility of healthy development.

The Seven Life Processes in Education

The subject of the seven life processes in education is very interesting because it highlights a child's physical and etheric foundation. Even with the best intentions and the cleverest methods for teaching children, one cannot get around the question of children's ability to receive what is being offered in education. That is why this topic is vitally important in the first seven years of childhood, during which the seven life processes find their way into the physical organism, consolidate themselves, and thereafter slowly free themselves from their purely body-forming functions. It is necessary to pay attention to and respect how the seven life processes are released from being exclusively bound to the physical body and transformed into soul faculties. For education that promotes health in body, soul, and spirit, it is important to examine a child's physical and etheric foundation. This is also the reason Waldorf education puts so little demand upon children's potential intellectual capabilities in the first seven years of childhood. Rudolf Steiner made reference many times to the metamorphosis of the etheric formative forces around the seventh year of life. He made it clear that making demands upon these released etheric forces too early would have a weakening effect on the still-developing physical body. Relative to this, we gain a greater conceptual clarity if we try to differentiate the etheric aspects from the viewpoint of the seven life processes. The birth of the etheric body shows itself as a process by which the seven life processes, influenced by seven different aspects, are activated through permeation into the physical body. Thus an illuminating connection can be made between the central anthroposophical insight into the seven-fold life streaming through us, and the knowledge of the birth of the etheric body around the time of the change of teeth, which is indispensable for education, particularly kindergarten education.

Metamorphosis of Etheric Formative Forces and the Release of Life Processes from Physical Bonds

The preceding descriptions of each of the life processes clearly indicate how they find their way into the body over the course of childhood. We learned how inside the body, the life processes become autonomous and individualized and how the forces that anchor these processes in the body are gradually released as soul faculties ready to be used by a human being. When everything "functions" as it should, a person is absolutely in control of these faculties. In cases of illness, deficient regeneration from lack of sleep, or excessive physical, emotional, or intellectual demands, these soul faculties are diminished because the etheric forces are needed for the maintaining of the physical body.

This correlation can be observed daily in young children during the so-called midday slump, when bile production is highest and the blood (and with it the "I") is somewhat more concentrated in the torso. Between two and three o'clock in the afternoon the etheric body is most strongly occupied with building and maintaining the physical body, apart from its regenerative activities during the night, of course. Temperature in the limbs decreases and internal body temperature in the torso increases (Hildebrandt, 1976). The stomach and intestines are working in high gear, as lunch has to be digested, and after the first high-performance period of midmorning around 10 am, the body needs a little regeneration phase in order to meet the demands of the next high-performance period (around 5 pm) with full energy. Practical life experience has taught almost everyone that the following things are more difficult in the early afternoon: attentiveness, concentration, interest and enthusiasm for something new, absorbing and making an inner connection with certain types of tasks, analytical thinking and sorting thoughts, remembering, practicing and perfecting skills, and forming ideas. Here we see how every day the connection between the seven life processes and the identified soul faculties is noticeable. Whenever the seven life processes turn to physical regeneration, at night and less intensely during the midday slump, the soul faculties arising from them are noticeably diminished.

The anchoring of the life processes that occurs during the first seven years, as was explained in previous chapters, determines the unfolding of specific soul faculties. These form the basic preconditions of soul necessary for extrinsic learning, and thus school readiness.

Since here we are dealing with the living structures of a human organism and not a machine, it becomes problematic if our thinking about a single soul faculty being attributed to a single life process is too static or inflexible. We should picture rather a tableau of soul faculties, such as concentration, interest, organization, memory, and practice, which are achieved if the seven life processes are able to be anchored in the body during early childhood. It is analogous to reaching a high plateau with a distant view of a hiking path into the mountainous heights, with plenty of ups and downs in-between. To further belabor the metaphor, on top of the high plateau are found the following faculties:

Perception	
Attention	*Breathing*
Concentration	
Interest	*Warming*
Enthusiasm	
Inner Connection	*Nourishing*
Selection and Sorting	
Arrangement and Organization	*Secreting*
Differentiation	
Questioning	
(Re)integration	*Maintaining*
Memory	
Practice, Improving	*Growing*
Expansion	
Idea Formation	*Producing – Reproducing*

Each of the life processes stands in a living relationship with these unfolding soul faculties. Physical breathing has special influence on lung activity, blood circulation, and heart function. The soul faculties associated with breathing have to do with perception and attention. At the same time, the way a person breathes has an influence on physical digestion and, regarding soul faculties, is associated with being able to make an inner connection with something.

Similarly, for example, physical secretions mainly have to do with sorting or elimination and soul-wise with differentiation, organization, and questioning. At the same time, secretions also have a strong influence on body warmth, through perspiration; the soul correlations are the faculties of perception, interest, memory, and so on.

Naturally, awareness of these things has to have consequences for education. If the faculties of concentration and enthusiasm have been released, then completely different subjects can be introduced to a child at this time than in early childhood. Early childhood education should be much more strongly focused on not hindering integration of the seven life processes into the physical body.

> It needs to be strongly emphasized that around the seventh year, approximately, of course, when the change of teeth occurs, there is a complete transformation, a complete metamorphosis in the life of a child. In a certain way, a child becomes a different being because of the change of teeth. What is the basis for this transformation in the being of a child? It is based upon the fact that in the seventh year those forces which were previously active as organic developmental forces that provided impulses for breathing, blood circulation, physical formation of the organism, and growth and nourishment, now leave only a portion of these forces behind for organic activity. The rest of these forces go through a metamorphosis; they change into a transformed soul life for the child, if I may put it that way. (Steiner, *Waldorf Education and Anthroposophy*, GA 304a)

The implications of such anthroposophical knowledge for education from early childhood through school age should now become a main topic of consideration. Lesson plan creation should also take into account the above-mentioned fluctuation in capacities during the day. However, in this regard, it is important to go deeper with our thoughts into the metamorphosis of the etheric forces.

The etheric body is a living power structure that creates the physical body, transforms it, and, after the seventh year, preserves and regenerates it. A human being comes into this world as an infant with physical structures inherited from its ancestors, but these structures are only conditionally suitable for the karmic intentions gained by the individuality between death and a new birth. These intentions led to a very specific soul constitution, a very specific configuration of the astral body, with which the individuality clothed itself on the way to incarnation. In accordance with karmic intentions and the configuration of the astral body, those living formative forces necessary for implementation of the pre-birth will are pulled in from the etheric world; included are all living thoughts of organ forms and functions, all other living functions, building up the human skeleton and sensory system, and so on. These are the living thoughts of a real and effective world of life — not abstract human ideas, but real, working thought forces that are drawn into the etheric body in such a way that they are suited to the incarnating individuality (see Steiner, GA 218). One person will surround himself more with the energy of conveyed thoughts which form the basis for formation of the metabolic-limb system, while another will go more with the thought forces which allow the nerve-sense system processes to emerge. This is why human beings have different and distinct strengths and weaknesses, also when it comes to the development of single organs. Lastly, the individuality, astral body, and etheric body clothe themselves with a physical body at conception, which develops in a mother's womb for nine months and is then born.*

Now begins the work of the etheric body on the inherited physical body so that later the adult person will resemble herself more than her parents. That is to say, she will more resemble her pre-birth intentions. (By the way, making this possible is one of the tasks of education!) The transformation of the physical body is completed with the help of the seven life processes. Without living processes a child would die immediately after birth. Breathing, warming, nourishing, etc. are necessary for these physical transformation processes to even be possible. The individual strength of each of the life processes, the predominance of certain life processes as opposed to others in individuals, is, again, the result of varying degrees of intensity with the "sheathing" of active thoughts from the etheric world, such as those of breathing or growing, for example. Not only are there individual differences in the formation of the physical body, but also in the structure of the seven life processes. It is true that all the processes are present in the

---

* A more exact and nuanced presentation of these connections relative to the nine-fold constitution of a human being is found in Rudolf Steiner's work, *Theosophy* (GA 9, Dornach 2003), in the chapters titled "The Essential Nature of Man" and "Reincarnation and Karma." Here it is explained how the etheric body and the soul body (not the astral body!), although supersensible in nature, originate in heredity and join with the three soul members (sentient soul, mind soul and consciousness soul) which in turn join with the three higher, spiritual members (spirit-self, life-spirit and spirit-man). Something similar is also presented in the first lecture of Rudolf Steiner's *Study of Man* (GA 293). Regardless, what was said above is fully justified because, first, it considers these connections from the viewpoint of the more easily understood four-fold nature of a human being, consisting of physical body, etheric body, astral body (cohabitation of soul-body and sentient body) and the "I"; and second, it considers that a human being does not incarnate into a hereditary lineage, with one or the other etheric characteristics, without a reason. This is connected with the development of karma (see Rudolf Steiner, *Geistige Zusammenhänge in der Gestaltung des menschlichen Organismus*, GA 218).

physical body from birth, but not yet to a degree that would allow a child to develop without care and nurturing.

These seven life processes, along with the living thoughts of individual forms, functions, structures, and organizations of the human body, only slowly and incrementally incarnate into the physical-material aspect; so that, as seen in the passage above by Rudolf Steiner, it is true that with the beginning of the change of teeth, life processes are released for soul activities. They are released because over the period of the first seven years they have anchored themselves deeper and deeper into the physical body so that the energy made possible through the anchoring process is now free for use by the soul. What remains in the physical body is only the *capability*, or *function*, of breathing, nourishing, growing, etc. The life process which brought these functions into the body is now able to develop as a soul faculty; but the faculties resulting from the incarnation, the anchoring, and thus from the release of the seven life processes, are not the only soul faculties a human being possesses. The thought formed by the heart is released when the heart functions autonomously; a part of the heart-nature is released. The formative forces which allow the form and function of a specific organ to come about are also released when the organ has matured. For example, the thought formed by the nerves is released, and, according to how protected or openly they are situated, determines the degree of nervousness in a human being.

From this perspective, the "birth" of the etheric body is the transformation of etheric formative forces and formation processes into soul forces and processes, of which the seven life processes are only a part. Therefore, the metamorphosis that occurs in a human being around the seventh year results from soul forces which have been released for the soul's use after completion of physical body formation. The formative energy of the living, etheric world of thoughts *and* the forces in the seven life processes are partially released. These new soul forces bring about the metamorphosis that takes place when a child transitions from kindergarten into school, which finds its conclusion in morphogenesis (coming into form), when the limbs have been transformed and individualized and the permanent teeth appear. The permanent teeth are made of the hardest material in the human physical body and are an indication that the life forces are no longer exclusively occupied with building up the physical body, but rather have now turned to the development of the soul. It requires only a small remainder of etheric thoughts and only the physical functions of the seven life processes in the body to continue to maintain and regenerate it, supply it with air and warmth, and make sure that the organs do not deviate from the form in which the living thoughts have created them. The etheric formative forces and life processes disappear completely from the permanent teeth once they have come in. If the teeth are destroyed, there is no possibility of healing from the physical body.

The release of etheric formative forces and disengagement of the seven life processes from their exclusively physical orientation are what make it possible for a human being to go through a metamorphosis. The release of soul faculties from out of the seven life processes after successful anchoring in the physical body is, strictly speaking, not yet metamorphosis. However, that which results from the release of these soul faculties and other etheric formative forces is most certainly metamorphosis: namely, the transformed physical form and soul constitution of a school-age child.

During the further course of youth, a human being goes through a metamorphosis a second and third time: first the astral body is "born" at the beginning of sexual maturity, and then the "birth" of the "I" happens in conjunction with the transition into early adulthood. Subsequently, the soul faculties released through the birth of the etheric body also come under the influence of the astral body and the "I." With nourishing comes the faculty of skeptical deconstruction, with secreting the faculties of analysis, questioning, and subjective judgment, and with reproduction comes the formation of great social ideas and the discovery of ideals, in conjunction with physical sexual maturity. These are examples of the soul faculties gained in connection with the birth of the astral body.

There is more on this topic below under "Salutogenic Teaching – Nurturing the Life Processes in School."

Nurturing the Seven Life Processes during the First Seven Years

With rapid, shallow breathing a three-year-old child comes into the kindergarten and quickly jumps from one play corner to another, paints a picture in thirty seconds, and is oblivious to what adults around him are saying. The same child comes into the kindergarten two-and-a-half years later when he is almost six years old. He calmly walks through the door, takes a deep breath, goes to the workbench and continues working for thirty minutes on the boat he started yesterday. He is able to rasp and file very evenly and pays attention to what he is doing.

This example clearly shows that during the course of the first seven years there are many changes in the relationship of breathing to soul faculties such as perception, endurance, and attention.

But what is required of parents and teachers if they wish to support this process through the healthy anchoring of the breathing process in the physical body? In the first period of life much depends on allowing a child to grow into a well-ordered daily routine, with a great deal of attention and care. There should be bright, alert daytime hours occupied with meal preparation and physical care (diaper changes, bathing, applying lotion, etc.) and calm, dark nighttime hours for sleeping. The younger a child is, the more she will determine the daily routine. She may want to breastfeed more often than parents would wish in regard to a regular routine, and perhaps she awakens more often at night. During the first year, and more strongly in the second and third years, a child increasingly experiences regular mealtimes, bedtimes, and repeated rituals like singing, praying, and story time, as steady reoccurrences of the familiar. Through this a sense of security is attained.

If the structure of the daily routine is supported by the familiar highlights of mealtimes and rituals, then the time in between these fixed points, during which all of the daily activities of the household are carried out, can be configured rhythmically. It is of benefit to young children when the daily time structure can rhythmically "breathe" and does not change every day. For instance, going to the market, or for a walk in the woods, could always take place the first thing after breakfast, while the later morning might be filled with some other household tasks while the child plays in the protective surroundings of the house. Or, the time after breakfast could be devoted to housework and indoor play and the later morning could include time spent outdoors. Similar basic time structures could also be applied to the afternoon hours. It really has nothing to do with creating inflexible or pedantic daily routines, which does rather more harm than good. The daily routine should be an external role model for dynamic breathing. Breathing is never fixed, but rather it is elastic and flexible. It has to do with a daily rhythm, not a daily beat.

In a Waldorf kindergarten this need is often acknowledged by allowing time for free play indoors before having a morning snack together. The time after the snack is often spent outdoors in the yard or playground. This is repeated every day. Here is also an opportunity for kindergartners (from about age three-and-a-half onward) to fully participate not only in the change from day to night and inside to outside, but also the changes between going outside for free play and coming back inside for finger games, circle games and meals; then returning outside once more for free play before coming back inside for a story and possibly lunch in the kindergarten. The moment the "I" consciousness has awakened during the course of the third year with subsequent attacks of "the terrible twos," it is possible to approach a child's soul with the simplest forms of culture. This is also when there begins to be agreement with coming inside and going outside at times other than in connection with mealtimes. In the chapter on breathing, we described the first step when attentiveness appears alongside perception; this could also be called *kindergarten readiness*. One has to be especially careful that this faculty of attentiveness is not instilled in children through the daily routine in kindergarten, or, perish the thought, through verbal reprimands. Attentiveness should be allowed to develop in early childhood from a rhythmic daily routine. This faculty may be used and cultivated, but it may not be summarily produced through education.

The background for all these considerations is the knowledge that children in the first seven years of life are mainly imitative beings. Not only do they imitate movements, speech, thinking, individual gestures, and facial expressions, but also everything that is in their surroundings, and that includes every kind of rhythm. There are the rhythms of nature, with light during the day and darkness at night — which have a strong influence on the release of hormones that are dependent upon the time of day (Ackerman, 2008) — as well as the larger rhythms of the year, with its great breathing arc: inhalation during winter and exhalation during summer. Every single day also has its own rhythms. All of this is imitated, agreed with, and participated in, unconsciously. It is participation in that which is immediately present. This faculty of imitation remains for one's whole life but it recedes in the wake of other approaches to the world. A school child also imitates, but as she gets older it is no longer so obvious because imitation steps into the background behind a self-chosen, beloved authority figure.

Through imitation, there is inner agreement and participation with the breathing life process for the simple reason that this life process is present in nature and can be cultivated by human beings. For anyone who has anything to do with young children, this knowledge should challenge us to consciously nurture the breathing life process. We are also called upon to pay especially close attention to the transitions from one activity to the next so that the flow of breathing during the day does not falter. Before a child reaches school age the breathing life process is not yet consolidated in the physical body, and thus abrupt transitions have a harmful influence on physical breathing and rhythmic blood circulation, that is, breathing and circulation without slow-downs or congestion. Such transitions include changing abruptly from playing to tidying up, singing to eating, painting to gardening, and so on. Just as voice pitch, gait, certain gestures, and other subtleties in children's surroundings are immediately imitated, in the same way children are internally deeply moved by that which is "breathing" in the configuration of space and time. Integration and anchoring of the breathing life process depends very much upon these factors. It is already clear what great responsibility actually lies with parents and kindergarten teachers. The harmonious integration of the breathing process, that is, the rhythmic formation of the physical body, provides the foundation for learning aptitude later on. If, because of insufficient stimulation, imitation of breathing processes does not occur, then the breathing life process cannot become deeply enough connected to the physical body and consequently cannot be adequately released for soul faculties. It is "physical education" in the highest sense.

This also can take us further than planning daily routines and experiencing the seasons of the year. All rhythmic household and handwork activities belong in a child's environment: washing, kneading, sawing, rasping, threshing, sweeping, digging, chopping, spinning, knitting, and so on. These activities may be sometimes fast and sometimes slow, just as with breathing. Songs, sounds, verses, poems, dancing, jumping…all must be included in order to learn right breathing.

"One should not underestimate the organ-building power found in dancing to musical rhythms," Steiner said in *The Education of the Child* (GA 34). And, one should not underestimate how much the connection between the "I" and the world created in this way leads to superior health of the soul. In the theory of Salutogenesis this is referred to as having a sense of coherence (Antonovsky, 1997).

Bringing basic rhythmic activities such as seemingly old-fashioned circle and singing games into a young child's environment is actually a conscious process, arising from the knowledge that a child needs these things in order to achieve a healthy physical body from which healthy soul faculties are able to develop. It has nothing to do with nostalgia, and the modern achievements of technology will not lose their value because of it. It is quite simply the task of education to make it possible to experience rhythm. The ability to grapple with the technical innovations in our world in a focused way will later develop out of this experience of rhythm.

The greatest educational challenge today is discovering a feeling for the many overlapping rhythms. If as an educator I rigidly follow a daily routine that has been worked out in one set of circumstances, then the children may not be able to adequately experience the seasons of the year as a great arc of breathing in nature. At home and in the kindergarten it may be thoroughly justified to spend significantly more time outdoors in the summer and more time in the comfort of indoors in the winter. The same goes for the tempo in singing songs, the length of midday naps, and so on. Additionally, there are the festivals and other exceptional times when it is all right if everything is a little different; also the fact that one rhythm will be right for one child while another needs something else. For many children it may be perfectly fine to begin play indoors at home or in the kindergarten in order to start their day warmly enveloped in aesthetic surroundings and household activities. Others are overwhelmed by the closeness of a room and learn better breathing if they can first go outdoors and run off some energy and then find their way back to the indoor space. As educators keeping these issues in mind, it is extremely difficult, but necessary, for us to act according to the needs of each child.

The rhythms described in the chapter on breathing are the basis for a child's physical development. If we were aware of just how much a person's aptitude for learning after the change of teeth depends upon the possibility of imitating, in a living way, all the rhythms — seasonal experiences, daily routine, singing, dancing — in early childhood, then this knowledge about bodily and cosmic rhythms would flow into practical life activities.

Actually, the ideal could be achieved in the musicality present in the sequential nature of things. The day, the week, the year all measure time in an unchanging beat. In contrast, the rhythms of going indoors and outdoors, inside and outside, being serious and silly do not always have to be the same. After all, the most beautiful works of music are not boring marches! And individual activities, those things that children learn through play, and that adults do very practically, are like a melody.

In this way a morning at a Waldorf kindergarten could be like a pleasant symphony with opposing melodies and repeated themes, including an overture and a final chord.

A child comes into the kindergarten with cold hands and is pale until after the morning snack. Only after going outside does he have red cheeks and is able to actively listen and follow the story at midday. Another child also comes into the kindergarten with cold hands, but she has to take off her sweater after fifteen minutes because she is too warm. She is happy to help mill the grain and set the table.

These examples highlight the differences in a body's ability to produce warmth and show the connection between warmth production and interest in happenings in the surroundings. As was shown in the chapter on warming, a young child's warmth is at first constantly flowing out so that it is difficult to protect against environmental temperatures. Over the course of the first seven years, a child matures from an infant who needs a protective hat even in summer, to a school child who can run barefoot through the snow and right afterwards have warm feet.

How are we able to support the process of integration of the warming life process into the physical body in the first seven years at home and kindergarten so that, as a result of a firm anchoring of the warmth process, soul faculties including interest, concentration, enthusiasm, and adaptability can be released?

Just as with integration of the breathing process, here we must also present ideals of warmth in external spaces for a child's imitating soul. The warming life process is able to anchor itself in the physical body in a healthy way if a child is able to imitate warming and cooling in the surroundings, as well as healthy adaptation to temperatures and social situations.

As has already been mentioned, the first step is to provide warm clothing and real, loving interest. Naturally, as far as loving interest, attentiveness, acceptance, and appreciation are concerned, the dependency upon external warmth regulation remains of significance for a person's entire life. This is also the only way bonds are created! Of course, in the physical, material sense, this dependency weakens over the course of childhood. By age three to five the child is able to cover up at night or remove covers by himself, and as he gets older is able to choose appropriate clothing; in other words, he has achieved a healthy sense of his own temperature comfort level.

The next step for healthy integration of the warming life process is providing "role models" of external warmth production. Such representative ideals will be experienced first of all everywhere there is physical warmth, and, secondly, wherever there is an experience of real enthusiasm. If cooking and baking at home or in kindergarten are done *in front of children* and not hidden away, it has an immediate health-giving effect on the anchoring of the warming process, especially if it requires actions like lighting a match to turn on a gas cooking stove and not simply pushing buttons on a microwave. This is an exemplary way of allowing a child to follow the warming process. Of course, it would be best to do things like lighting a candle, making a fire, turning on the oven, and allowing the bread to rise in front of and with the children.

The warming of the body that takes place with physical work also belongs to this category of role models. There is nothing more stimulating than experiencing another person in the process of creating warmth. An adult doing physical work in the form of crafts, sweeping, carrying boxes, gardening, and so on is a healthy example for a child's physical body. This stimulus has an especially healthy effect if the worker's strength is not perceptibly overtaxed — as shown by sweat pouring down his face and heavy breathing. A healthy amount of effort, with adequate breaks in between, is something that a child is able to imitate.

The second model for warmth production is the amount of concentration and enthusiasm adults bring to their activities. The child's need for experiencing enthusiasm in others touches on the question of self-education. As a mother, father or kindergarten teacher, should I do everything which is said to be meaningful for a child? Or should I think about what I enjoy, for which I can display true interest and enthusiasm? Rather than being put through a well-intentioned "Waldorf program" of watercolor painting, eurythmy, knitting, crocheting, and gnome stories, all done without enthusiasm, it would be healthier for a child to experience only those things in which adults are also truly interested. It is very possible that a mother or father has no special affinity for the ritualized lighting of a candle before meals or bedtime. In that case, it is best not to do it! It could also happen that a kindergarten teacher is not enthusiastic about knitting or crocheting, in which case it would be better to create some other kind of activity instead of allowing the children to sense one's lack of interest.

Another question arises of whether I, as an adult, am really interested in anything outside of my pedagogical role as mother, father or kindergarten teacher. Enthusiasm for an ideal or interest in an activity with a specific theme creates a health-promoting environment for children. The activity does not necessarily need to have anything to do with education or child development; enthusiasm as a principle and with its potential for producing warmth of soul can then be perceived by a child.

A further point is the question of presenting models for the faculty of adaptability. If a child's organism has to learn how to maintain temperature and react accordingly to external warming or cooling, then models are important here as well so that soul and social adaptability can develop. The more adults are able to come to agreement, show true interest in the needs of others, and remain open to compromise (even when children are not watching) — in short, the more they carry out their social lives on the basis of warmth of soul — the more children in such an environment will develop into socially adaptable human beings with a healthy sense for social processes.

A child sits at the breakfast table but will not eat anything. Later, in kindergarten, she remains a little on the outside of things the whole day and is only sporadically able to become immersed in free play. She eats very well at lunch but does not chew her food well and after a long period of reluctance is finally able to move around joyfully on an afternoon walk. Another child ate a little muesli in the morning, enjoys the morning in the kindergarten, and is able to say exactly how much millet porridge he would like ("middle"). Outdoors, he plays non-stop and cheerfully switches roles many times in the games the children are playing.

These examples show the connection between nourishment and the ability of the soul to receive things and form bonds and connections. A child who eats healthfully and shows a sense for the right amount of food is in a position to fully and completely receive things that are in the environment. On the other hand, a child who has problems with eating breakfast and does not chew food properly takes a long time to find something she can connect with. Her nourishment processes are (even now) more concerned with making sure the physical nourishment process is able to be at all successful. Such observations should not lead us to make value judgments on children and their differences, but rather to recognize of the behavior as it relates to the life process, which in turn can help us to better understand each child.

Healthy education at home and in kindergarten depends on providing adequate model examples. In this way the life process can be so strongly anchored through nourishment that enough forces can be released for the soul to develop the faculties of receiving and connecting. In later childhood, the more the nourishing life process has to deal with enabling the physical nourishment process, the less the soul will be able to receive and make inner connections with the things of the world. If, however, during the course of the first seven years nourishment as a physical function is firmly anchored in the organism through adequate stimulation, then enough soul forces can be released to enable the soul to be receptive to the world and to form inner connections.

Now, the focus must be on adequate stimulation. The first question that arises is: what constitutes healthy nutrition in infancy and early childhood? If food is of the best quality and demands neither too little nor too much from the organism, then a good foundation for continuing support of this life process has been established.

In practice, this means, first of all, avoidance of non-organic food, since pesticide residues and farmland that is lacking in vital, living substance cannot provide adequate support for children's physical bodies and their system of life forces, and could be harmful. Besides this, there should be a healthy variety of fruits and vegetables consisting of root vegetables (carrots, parsnips, red beets, for example), leaf and stem vegetables (spinach, Swiss chard, fennel, rhubarb, etc.) and fruit, as well as a modest amount of whole grain products. The different types of vegetables and fruits have different effects on the body's nerve-sense, rhythmic and metabolic-limb systems (see the chapter on "nourishing"). Whole grains contain very important life-promoting substances, which are almost completely missing from white, processed flour. In order to avoid overburdening the physical organism, food has to be chopped or pureed, depending on a child's age. Because of the difficulty in digesting it, rye grain should be completely avoided at first, even in the form of bread.

One should also see to it that meals contain little sugar, salt, meat, and eggs. Instead, there should be plenty of milk products and premium-quality oils. In this way, from a physiological standpoint, one can achieve strengthening of the organism and a healthy medium between placing too little demand on the physical organism and overburdening it (see for example Kuehne, 2004).

Over and above the question of healthy nutrition, the first seven years have mainly to do with the principle of the nourishing process in the physical realm, but also providing exemplary representation of the soul-spirit aspect in external spaces. The principle of the nourishing life process — taking in nutrition, processing sensory impressions, and perceiving feelings and intellectual content — always involves merging together, making smaller, breaking down. Where can we experience something like that?

Merging substances together, as a principle, can be experienced when raking leaves in the yard, gathering flowers for a bouquet from different areas of the garden, or dumping together different play materials, for example. The principle of making substances smaller can be experienced while cutting fruit, picking through wool, or chopping wood. The principle of breaking down substances can be experienced by heating beeswax until it melts, changing its structure, or through experiencing the smells of cooking food that are released through a chemical process, in which case the interplay between the nourishing and secreting processes is highlighted once again.

Experiences of work that involve the processes of merging together, making smaller, and breaking down substances are naturally extremely valuable. This is the case with making applesauce, for example: First the apples are gathered and put together in a bowl. They are sliced (made smaller) and then taken from different cutting boards and put back together in a cooking pot. Then they are heated, whereby there is a chemical change in the structure of the apples; they become soft and porridge-like and give off a stronger aroma than before.

This kind of stimulation, in conjunction with healthy and relaxed eating, contributes to the strengthening of the life process of nourishing. There is exemplary experience of what a nourishing process is, and if the food is healthy and mealtimes stress-free, then the nourishing process can be thoroughly exercised. This is how the foundation is laid for the soul faculties of receptiveness and making inner connections, which develop out of the nourishing process.

But there is one thing that should not be forgotten: how does a child experience me as a mother, father, or kindergarten teacher? Do I eat with calm and enjoyment? Does my normal diet include fast food or special diet foods? Do I listen to my surroundings and really take in what others are saying? Do I fully connect with whatever I am doing at the moment, or am I always thinking about the next thing? With this, the question of the self-education of model-providing adults is again highlighted. Being truly receptive and making connections with the surroundings is a process that is present in space, and it will be imitated exactly the same as cooking applesauce or one's own eating behavior. This is, then, a soul process; however, it works on the formation of the physical body and life structures in the same way as the physical-spatial processes. Any parent who has practiced even a little self-observation knows that one's own inner flightiness, as well as lack of perceptual ability (breathing) and failing interest (warming), can be read in children's behavior. What it comes down to is exemplifying in your own life the physical processes of receiving, making smaller, and breaking down substances, as well as the soul process of making inner connections with your surroundings.

During a visit with relatives, a two-year-old child eats goulash with noodles for the first time and suffers irregular digestion in the following days. Climbing stairs and bedtime becomes more difficult than usual and the parents wonder why their child is so grumpy. In contrast, the child's ten-year-old sister has spent the last few days learning about Norse mythology from her class teacher and has asked her parents several times how the Norse creation myth and the story of Adam and Eve in the Bible can go together. In spite of the goulash and the immense ash tree, Yggdrasil, her digestion remains unchanged.

This family's example shows how much a two-year-old's feelings of well-being are tied to the physical body. Because of his age, the two-year-old's physical organism is not yet able to correctly sort food that is difficult to digest. On the other hand, his big sister's physical organism has learned to sort things in a healthy way; that applies to food as well as sensory impressions. By the time a child is ten years old the secreting processes work so autonomously that neither goulash nor the irritation of having an accepted concept of creation brought into question by Norse creation mythology has any effect on the physical organism. A strong foundation has been established so that now it is possible, through thinking, to attempt to bring the biblical and Norse creation stories into harmony. A child does not have to simply capitulate in the face of chaotic thoughts, but is able to actively practice bringing order into the soul aspect.

Regarding the secreting life process, what is meant, among other things, is the sorting and ordering of what was previously received. Intestinal activity during the digestion process brings this clearly to light. Before nutrients pass through the intestinal wall, certain substances are internally secreted and put at the disposal of the physical organism. As was explained in the chapter on the secreting process, this process is also involved in secretion of saliva, sweat and neurotransmitters during the transfer of nerve impulses. The secreting process is not limited to elimination, but includes every kind of excretion, "incretion," and sorting. It is the analyzing and organizing activity of the physical organism. When a child is ready for school, the soul faculties of ordering and sorting can develop because during the first seven years the physical body has taken hold of the secretion process. Differentiation is now gradually possible and the foundation has been laid for analytical thought at a later time.

Again, what this means for home and kindergarten during the first seven years is that this process should be exemplified in the external spaces so that a child is able to experience it. Because of a child's urge to imitate, external representative models of the secretion process have a beneficial influence on internal, physical organizational functions. Integration of the secreting process into a child's physical body leads to the release of etheric forces which then appear as the soul faculties of ordering and sorting.

What might such health-promoting models for the secretion process look like? In the home it helps if there is a clear order in the structures of space and time that a child is able to experience. Without being pedantic about it, in the first seven years it benefits children when the candle on the table is in the same place every day, the building blocks are put away in the same basket, the place where mother or father prepare meals is familiar from day to day and when the daily routine is consistent. A child experiences a health-promoting form of organization if the sequence of activities in the evening remains the same; dinner, brush teeth, put on pajamas, story time. Additionally, it is especially beneficial if the main, warm meal is not eaten sometimes at noon or sometimes in the evening. Having the main meal around the same time every day allows digestive habits to become anchored, thereby using less energy than if the stomach and intestines are "surprised" with new demands on a daily basis. (The liver-gallbladder rhythm, with its high point of bile production and reduction in body temperature in the limbs in the early afternoon, actually speaks in favor of having the hardest-to-digest meal at noon. This is because during the day etheric forces are more strongly involved in physical regeneration, and less so with the soul-related activities requiring concentration, interest, and so on.)

In the kindergarten, too, clearly structured time and space are good stimulants for the secreting life process. So are all activities of tidying up and organizing, especially if these are sometimes more exact in nature —

sorting all the towels by color, for instance. Giving one child a special role in the middle or inside or outside of the circle during circle games allows him to experience meaningful and aesthetic forms and structures.

One model of the secreting process that is particularly stimulating, especially for the digestive process, is to create order out of chaos. Naturally, this applies to the home as well. Gather up all the play materials used during the day, sort them out, and put everything in its proper place. Deconstructing a chaotic mess by folding cloth, rolling up ribbons, separating chestnuts from pinecones and putting them in their own baskets, and so on is a healthy model of internal organizational processes. Inside the body the "chaotic food mixture" is also efficiently utilized, with single elements either being incorporated into or eliminated from the physical organism.

If we take these thoughts about example and imitation seriously, then we should also consider how adults are utilizing a differentiated way of looking at things in the world. How do things stand with my own soul-spirit secreting processes? Do I bring everything into chaos or do I practice differentiation? If actions and expressions of individual children are not thrown all together into one pot, but considered individually, and if one's own approach to the world, independent from pedagogical issues, is imbued with a striving to differentiate various observed happenings and events, then children grow up in an environment in which things are meaningfully ordered, analyzed, and penetrated in a fundamental way. This is, in the truest sense, a "role-model" environment in which children will be able to develop their secreting processes.

A seven-year-old child is in bed with a fever and swollen tonsils. Her throat is red, food holds no appeal and when questioned about anything she reacts with a shoulder shrug. Three days later the swelling has gone down and the previous form is restored. The child remembers an exciting story her teacher had just begun to tell and she wants to hear the next part. The maintaining life process has reappeared after having been exclusively concerned with the physical body, but now the faculty of memory is able to continue to develop unhindered.

This example is good for observing the connection between the process of maintaining and the faculty of memory. Memory depends upon the body's healing processes being able to proceed autonomously; in other words, upon the maintaining process being able to anchor itself in the physical aspect during the first few years of life. Fevers and childhood illnesses have their necessary place here. A child *must* be allowed to experience her capability of self-healing in the first seven years. It is a fundamental prerequisite for developing the faculty of memory.

What might healthy stimulation for anchoring the maintaining process look like? Where can models of this process be experienced in the home and kindergarten? In repair work, in making something whole again; in everything having to do with maintenance and care of spaces and the materials contained in them. The more that activities like cleaning, polishing and mending happen with children present, the more beneficial it is for the physical development of the maintaining process and for the later capability of freely "calling up" memories because children imitate what they experience in the environment. Experiencing someone doing maintenance and repairs affects them all the way into their physical-etheric constitution during the first seven years. Even later there are still many effects from outwardly represented life processes. But, above all, the most physically formative, and transformative, effects come from the experiences children have before they start school. Even as adults, we have all experienced how restoring order in our personal spaces helps to sort out disorder in the soul.

Another important support for anchoring the maintaining process and the later capacity for memory is constant repetition of the same or similar processes. Recognition of a familiar daily routine, playing the same game over and over, having regular meals, doing specific activities that belong to certain days of the week, experiencing the seasons of the year and the festivals that accompany them, all lead to continuous maintenance of the wide variety of neuronal connections in the brain, as do all the constantly reappearing sensory impressions we experience. As was already explained in the chapter on maintaining, a one-time experience of different, related sense perceptions is not enough for them to be remembered later. The synaptic connections for single, interconnected nerve cells only become strong when the same or similar experiences are had daily, weekly, and yearly; and this is *really the only way*. Rhythmical recurring experiences not only benefit the breathing process through rhythmic repetition, but also the soul's maintaining capability. Memory, experience, and knowledge of associations of meaning are possible in later life because the maintaining process was able to strongly anchor itself in the structure of the brain. The preservation of sensory impressions of things of a similar nature, and of associations of meaning, has to be practiced daily over a period of years, even beyond the first seven years, in order to preserve experiences in the soul which can be remembered.

Therefore, it is the task of parents and early childhood educators to allow children to experience maintenance and repair work along with adults, and to allow them to experience repetitions of the same, or similar, activities so that a strong anchoring of the maintaining life process will be achieved.

For adults, what kind of example is being set when it comes to attention and care of the body, one's sense of life and one's own soul? Do the children live in an environment that is worthy of imitation, in which adults earnestly care for their own regenerative forces so much that they are a shining example for children? These questions are especially relevant in regard to adults' self-education, because then children will have available to them a soul-spirit space in which parents and kindergarten teachers truly strive for maintaining and regenerating.

A five-year-old boy's parents were surprised to find that his old shoes were too small and he already needed a size one. In kindergarten during the following months he built cranes and catapults outside over and over again whereby he extensively trained his sense of balance and understanding for the trajectories of sand and rocks. Furthermore, he had the idea to add a humorous rhyming word to everything his kindergarten teacher said. His eleven-year-old sister has recently become part of a young people's circus and practices riding a unicycle for half an hour every day, even though she can already ride very well.

This example shows us the connection between physical growth and the ability to practice something. The five-year-old boy's play is gradually extended and the eleven-year-old girl is totally self-motivated to further improve her skill.

At home or in kindergarten, one can tell by the way children attempt to expand their skills and abilities from out of their own selves just how far the growing process has metamorphosed, or to what extent its effects are still bound up with the physical body. Composing additional lyrics to songs, working on simple activities such as weaving or sewing, or as in the example above, coming up with rhymes belong in this category.

In the kindergarten children are able to experience the long-term growing process in a garden when adults consciously care for it through the seasons. Also, the experience of progress in some kind of continuous activity such as weaving or finger-crocheting assures the external presence of the growing life process.

If we follow the idea that through imitation children of kindergarten age not only receive actions and words into themselves, but also the processes which are used to form the physical body and its vital functions, it stands to reason that for later soul expansion and the ability to practice and continually strive for improvement, much depends upon whether growing, as a process, is experienced in the first seven years of life.

Furthermore, much will depend upon whether a child's growth and stages of development are perceived and recognized by adults. A lively, constantly-active two-year-old, a stubborn three-year-old, or a five-year-old whose arms have grown so long that he bangs into things all over the place — all require understanding, recognition and confidence. In short, they require love for each and every condition of growth. Growth in body and soul needs loving interest, for otherwise there is a danger that a child will not be able to live up to behavioral "demands." A lack of joy in practicing, failure, and repeated attempts can be the result. The release of soul faculties which comes from a healthy anchoring of the growing processes does not only depend upon having representations of growth and becoming in the external environment. Adults who follow the growing process with interest and attentiveness provide support for children.

Besides growth in a child's body and increased efficiency of the internal organs, there is also gradual growth in the ability to interact with groups. Therefore, necessary protection from excessive social demands is also part of the care and support for the growing life process. Faculties and abilities are born; they cannot be trained into a person. Just as the soul's ability to practice, expand, and strive for improvement arises from physical growth, so also is the ability to survey and comprehend social situations only gradually released as a result of physical growth. A child near the end of kindergarten, who has grown tall, has no more baby paunch, and tests out the world with coordinated, relatively thin limbs, physically illustrates the ability to survey and comprehend in the form of a longer neck. The head has distanced itself from the torso, which goes along with the child's developing eagerness for learning, imagination, and the capability of sitting together with a large class. This also illustrates some problems in the way kindergartens and, especially, daycare settings are currently conceptualized and organized. Because of the number of children in these groups (up to fifteen children in daycare groups and up to twenty-five children in kindergarten groups), situations arise that are not always in accordance with the social skills of the corresponding age groups.

The question for adults regarding their own self-education is: Am I expanding my skills and faculties enough or is my behavior merely routine? Am I really a role model for soul growth and the will to practice and improve? Those who always seek to improve their skills, grapple with the unknown, and, most especially, find the courage to admit their own imperfection, lack of skill or finesse, create an environment for children in which it is all right to practice something that one is not yet very good at. "I need to practice!" is an expression that can hardly be overused around young children.

However, bear in mind that something can be practiced in a sensible way only if it does not completely overtax you. It is healthy to expand according to your own individual possibilities and not chase after unreachable goals. Just as the life processes always work in harmony in the physical organism, the soul faculty of practice also requires a basis of strength that allows it to develop. Nothing can grow without breathing, nourishing, and maintaining. In the same way, I do not feel like practicing something if I am unable to concentrate or make a connection with it.

Something that is also decisive here is the motive of one's own method of practice. If what I practice is to fulfill a specific convention or norm (even if it is a "good" Waldorf habit), I am no longer the author of my own actions. In contrast, if my motive to practice is totally my own then I am a role model for individual growth. Transformation of the inherited physical body in a child's first seven years can become all the more individual if adults' motives for practicing activities, expanding their abilities, or changing established habits come from within and not from without.

A five-year-old kindergartner was conspicuous because she never had any ideas of her own for play and usually just went along with the others. She was normally adaptable, and when not, it was with an attitude of refusal. A routine examination by her doctor showed she was slightly deficient in red blood cell formation. In contrast, another child, who had just turned seven, was never lacking ideas for play and had already surprised his kindergarten teacher with many of his "ideas," which have given him a reputation for being impertinent, but also cute.

It is astounding how few ideas of their own young kindergarteners are able to develop. Usually, they merely appropriate and implement outside suggestions. At the same time, it is also clear that the great social ideas are not able to be born in the first school years, but rather only with the onset of puberty, when the reproducing process has become active in maturing the sexual organs and is able to act autonomously in the body. In between, during the whole of the second seven-year period, it can be observed how school children no longer latch onto stimuli from the environment like kindergartners, especially the stimuli from the learning and social environment at school. Now, that which is seen and heard is implemented, but also changed and infused with their own ideas to a much higher degree than before. For instance, if a dramatic performance is seen in a theater it is not only imitated during play, but the idea of theatrical performance is taken up and filled with original ideas. One seldom sees this with kindergartners. Although they will create their own puppet plays, the dialogue is usually taken from something they have heard before. Sometimes children will not be able to think of any dialogue on their own. In that case it is up to adults to improvise something appropriate for the scenery and then narrate the puppet play.

It is clear that the producing process is mostly limited to the physical body when children are of kindergarten age. When you consider that inherited physical forms and functions first have to become individualized in the physical body (see also the section on "Production in the Soul and Spirit") it is understandable that kindergarten and home life must provide possibilities for the imitative child to experience the producing process. He or she will then be able to use these examples of creation in order to produce something from out of the self. If too much is expected from children, or they are encouraged too often to come up with their own ideas, they are pulled away from the formation of their physical body, which is not helpful for the process of individualization.

In kindergarten, the process of reproducing (or rather, producing) can best be experienced through sowing seeds, planting bulbs, and observing the development of plants. Creating something new within view of the children is also a good representation of this process — not only repairing something that was damaged (maintaining), but really making something new or completely replacing something old. A few examples of things that can be "produced" are candles, card stands, and weaving frames. It is also very easy to encourage production at home. Every homemade lantern, carved stick, or painted picture is something created by human beings and new to the world.

In this regard, the artistic activity of adults both at home and in the kindergarten assumes a very valuable role. If a child grows up in an environment in which paintings, music, and poetry are created, he is given an example of productive space that can be imitated. With this kind of stimulus, a child is better able to transform and individualize his inherited physicality. For kindergarten, this also means that original finger games, rhymes, and stories are of great benefit to children. Here also are implications for self-education in regard to the producing process. Where do I stand with my own, completely personal, artistic ideas? What is my personal opinion about burning social questions? What is my personal viewpoint on the societal problem-areas of education, family, work, and income? Am I merely parroting sound bites and snippets from talk shows and magazine articles, or am I led by my ideals? Do I have a primary motif that underlies my ideas and actions? Within the honest answers to these questions lies something that a child perceives in the soul environment, and that helps her to gradually place herself in the world as an individual.

The above suggestions for an external representation of the seven life processes through household activities and adult self-education have illustrated the influence of the seven life processes. Naturally, the ideal can only be for us to grasp, as far as possible, the "weaving in and out and on top of each other" nature of the seven life processes. In this way we may create an educational structure that bears within it as a model the side-by-side, simultaneous nature of the life processes in the physical organism.

This is the case with any kind of farming or gardening activity. Digging up a garden bed is a rhythmic activity (*breathing*). Then there are substances mixed into the soil (*nourishing*) and larger rocks or weed roots have to be sorted out and removed (*secreting*). The health of the soil is promoted (*maintaining*) and the *growing* and *reproducing* of plants made possible. Such activities exemplify how all the life processes pass through the physical organism with every single breath. In the same way, concentration, interest, inner connection, and so on should also simultaneously appear, because the ideal is certainly not to concentrate on something for which there is no interest. The organs of living faculties flow more in and out and on top of each other and are not sharply delineated from each other, unlike the physical sense organs. For this reason the soul faculties are also not so clearly separated from each other.

Conscious separation of the individual life processes and the resultant soul faculties is only necessary because we do not work in harmony with nature, in which realm we have all the life processes around us simultaneously. Our life and work involve specialized areas of expertise that came about because of our civilization's advancement into the division of labor. This is all well and good, and it could really be no different on the path to individual freedom because otherwise everyone would be trapped in the necessities of nature. However, the consequence is that education cannot address the question of individual life processes and their connections with soul faculties in a natural way, but only under conditions dictated by the culture. If there is a kindergarten located on a farm it is hardly necessary to consider how and when the life processes could be nurtured and stimulated, because all of the life processes are present in the environment all the time. It is satisfying to have confirmation that such a kindergarten would be extremely sensible from an anthroposophical point of view. However, in every other kindergarten, in cities or even smaller towns, these natural representations of the life processes, which would lead to firm anchoring of those same processes when children imitate them, are not to be found. Educators are challenged to consciously integrate the life processes back into everyday life in order to promote healthy and skillful bodies and souls in children.

Bringing this process of consciousness to completion is a great task of education, and our desire is to maintain awareness of this process: "Children do not simply want to mind and follow when someone tells them what to do. They want to imitate what adults are doing. So, it is the task of a kindergarten to bring in activities of everyday life in a form which allows them to flow into children's play by their own activity. One has to introduce life, the activities of life, into the activities of a kindergarten" (Steiner, *The Child's Changing Consciousness as the Basis of Pedagogical Practice*, GA 306).

If children are able to enjoy a living environment in which they are allowed to experience the seven life processes, they become immersed in the imagination-filled, musical, artistic world of thinking, learning, and memory known as the second seven-year period, with its widely diverse soul faculties.

> *If one super-sensibly observes a child in his seventh year, at the time of the change of teeth, it is as if, I would like to say, a supersensible, etheric cloud is stepping out. It contains the same forces that were still deeply immersed in the physical body up to the change of teeth and had functioned rather awkwardly in the child up to that time because they are not used to working in the physical body. But now, with the change of teeth, these forces become accustomed to working for their own purposes and only a part of these forces are sent down into the physical body. On the one hand, they function in growing, nourishing, etc. but they are also freely active in childhood imagination. They want to emerge at a higher level by way of love for things; for people. They are not yet functioning in the areas of intellect, reasoning and ideas. The soul in the etheric body has been released in the child. The child has become a fundamentally different being by going through the change of teeth. . . .*
>
> *Yes, what is it we are actually nurturing? We are nurturing the same forces which produce correct digestion, allow human beings to grow and, from childhood on, allow them to grow into great human beings; these forces make possible internal and external growth. And that which we nurture in the soul is actually only a counter-image of the growth forces* (Steiner, *Waldorf Education and Anthroposophy*, GA 304a).

In the following chapter we will deal with the education and cultivation of the "freed soul in the etheric body" and the "counter-images of growth forces." From the perspective of the seven life processes many things are possible in terms of salutogenic (health-promoting) teaching, from the way in which lessons are begun and concluded, to the creation of lesson plans.

Salutogenic Teaching: Nurturing the Seven Life Processes in School

The previous considerations about nurturing the life processes at home and kindergarten had to do with achieving firm anchoring of the life processes in the physical organism by way of imitation of external processes as well as the soul-disposition of adults. The suggested pedagogical actions and behaviors influence physical development in young children.

In school we are now dealing with what has resulted from the anchoring of the life processes in the physical body during the first seven-year period. If teachers notice that certain soul faculties such as concentration, enthusiasm, inner connection, or orderliness of soul have somewhat imperfectly developed from the anchoring of the seven life processes, in terms of further development it is especially desirable if the people who have anything to do with such children are adequately informed about early childhood education. If the ability to concentrate is lacking, the only viable approach (as long as you are not trying to introduce military-style drilling as an educational method) is to use still-lingering imitation abilities in order to strengthen the anchoring of the breathing life process by representing breathing, rhythmic processes in the children's environment.

The same approach also applies to the problem of lack of interest in school; here also it is necessary to present external examples of warmth production, enthusiasm, and participation so that the urgently needed faculties of interest, enthusiasm, and adaptability, which were apparently underdeveloped before reaching school age, can now develop from out of the anchoring of the warmth-production life process.

The same goes for the following processes: *nourishing* – inner connection; *secreting* – inner orderliness; *maintaining* – memory; *growing* – ability to practice and improve; *reproducing* – ideas and ideals. One should certainly not think that there is no more imitating going on in the second (or even the third) seven-year period simply because this faculty is now more in the background and the focus is on following a beloved authority figure. The faculty of imitation is merely overlaid by its successor. After puberty the faculty of judgment is superimposed onto the desire to follow an authority figure. Nothing disappears, but only steps a little into the background. Those who observe themselves and others may also notice adults' unconscious imitation of their surroundings (and authority figures as well). It is generally acknowledged that a school child's faculty of imitation is most pronounced before age ten. However, this should not prevent us from counting on the unconscious ability to imitate that accompanies us throughout our lives, as the advertising industry knows so well. In school much becomes possible if this one fact is consciously managed.

Here, at the beginning of the considerations about nurturing the life processes in school, we emphasize the importance of processes of work and production that are worthy of imitation.

Apart from the fact that continued focus on certain elements of kindergarten education in school can strengthen children's health of body and soul, how is a school able to become a place where children's newly "born" faculties (concentration, interest, inner connection, etc.) can be cultivated? Kindergarten has to do with the healthy development of the *physical body*, but later schooling is focused on healthy development of *soul faculties* released during the process of physical organ development.

Ask yourself: Do my lessons have a breathing quality? Is too little or too much concentration demanded? Are my lessons interesting and warming? Are the children able to make an inner connection; am I "nourishing" them enough? Is there something present to internally organize and make distinctions? Are there enough possibilities for remembering, for preserving in the soul that which has been? Do the children have enough space for practice, improvement, and soul growth? Am I adequately stimulating the formation of ideas, soul-spiritual production?

From the perspective of the seven life processes, these are very significant questions for teachers. Health of body, soul, and spirit is always the goal, so that a growing human being is able to make a strong, comprehensive connection to the world with as few limitations as possible. (By the way, "spiritual health" is actually a nonsensical term because the spirit can never be ill, although there may be physical, life-functional, or soul-related hindrances present.)

This is also a good explanation of the term "salutogenesis" (from the Greek words for "health" and "creation"). If our teaching is to be salutogenic, then, even as we nurture the life processes and the soul faculties resulting from them, we must strive toward what the latest discoveries in research on salutogenesis describe as *coherence*, with teaching that is meaningful, comprehensible, and manageable (Antonovsky, 1997).

In regard to the *breathing* life process and the faculty of perception that proceeds from it, it is very important that the school day as a whole and the individual lessons within it have a breathing quality. If the school day is to have meaning and rhythm then the first place to look is the class schedule. If the school subjects change at forty-five-minute intervals during the day, as well as from one day to the next, it can massively impair the faculty of perception because such a schedule is not based on any kind of energy-saving rhythm. The abrupt transitions from one subject to the next have to be balanced with a lot of effort, requiring concentration. This concentration is then lacking in other places, especially when the sequence of the subjects does not include a gradual transition from academic subjects to those involving physical movement. A sequence of subjects such as mathematics, physical education, English, handwork, biology, and music represents an extreme challenge to concentration and is even harmful to physical health, because each subject is unrelated to the one before.

Rudolf Steiner expressed his opinion about this problem very clearly. Consider his explanation about the connection between concentration and a rhythmic daily structure:

> If one wishes to educate, one also has to have a certain amount of elbow room. However, that is what one does not have if a dreadful class schedule is implemented in the customary way: Religion from 8 to 9, sports from 9 to 10, history from 10 to 11 and arithmetic from 11 to 12. In this case, everything that comes later cancels out what occurred previously. As a teacher, one can do nothing and may be brought to despair trying to cope with the situation. That is the reason we have something in the Waldorf School which could be referred to as block teaching. A child comes into class. Each day, during the all-important morning hours, from 8 to 10, or 8 to 11, the main lesson is taught as a consistent block with appropriate short breaks. One teacher is in the classroom, even in the upper grades. There are no hourly changes in subject. For whatever subject is being studied, arithmetic, for example, one would take 4 weeks, let us say, as a block of time spent on that subject during the main lesson. So, every day from 8 to 10, that particular subject is taught and the next day's lesson is always tied into what came the day before. There is no problem of later lessons canceling out previous lessons; concentration is possible. After four weeks have passed and the arithmetic block can be brought to a close, one begins with a history block which likewise lasts from four to five weeks, and so on (Steiner, *Human Values in Education*, GA 310).

And this about physical education activities followed by academic lessons:

> You see, during the time a human being is active in the metabolic-limb system, the thoughts which are artificially brought into the head between birth and death are then outside of the head. The child moves, jumps around; brings the metabolic-limb system into activity. The thoughts that have been planted during the physical life on Earth withdraw. But that which otherwise figures in dreams, a supersensible wisdom, is now in the head in an unconscious way and prevails

there. Therefore, if we bring a child back into the classroom after physical activity or sports, we are giving him something which, to his subconscious mind, is inferior to what he just had with the physical activity. During the physical activity it was not only the senses that had a pedagogical effect on the child, but also supersensible aspects were very strongly active during the physical activity. That is why the child will become internally unwilling during the following lesson in school. The child may not express it very strongly, but he will become internally unwilling. And we spoil things; we promote a tendency to illness in the child by grafting the regular school lessons onto some kind of physical education activity (Steiner, *Soul Economy*, GA 303, Lecture 6).

Additionally, in regard to creating a breathing-like structure for the school day, it is very important to clearly understand that human performance levels vary based on daily biological rhythms. Different studies have concluded that the human organism's performance levels are highest around 10 am and 5 pm and are lowest around 2 pm and 2 am (Glöckler, 1998). These results are supported by studies on reaction times, frequency of errors with shift workers and locomotive engineers, and falling asleep at the wheel (Hildebrandt, 1976). There is always an increase in such incidents from around 2 pm to 3 pm and from 1 am to 4 am, and corresponding high points of concentration in the morning and early evening.

However, it is not enough to plan the class schedule so that subjects are taught only until 1 pm and then resumed again in the late afternoon with further classes or perhaps homework assignments. There is another important difference between the morning and afternoon hours: the morning hours are better suited to addressing the nerve-sense pole in the human organism and the afternoon hours more suited to addressing the metabolic-limb pole. From self-observation one will notice that concentrated learning, absorbing intellectual content, is easier in the morning than in the afternoon.

This is supported by studies of the liver-gallbladder rhythm (see Bünning, 1977; Rosslenbroich, 1994; Schad, 1994). From approximately 2 pm onward the liver begins to build up the storage carbohydrate known as glycogen. This glycogen enrichment lasts until approximately 2 am. That is when the liver contains the highest amount of glycogen. Afterward, the process of decreasing glycogen in the liver begins; until 2 pm glycogen is released into the physical organism where it is turned into glucose in the bloodstream. It is true that the hormones insulin and glucagon maintain relatively constant blood sugar levels, but still, between the hours of 2 pm and 2 am the physical organism is busy building up stores of glycogen in the liver and between the hours of 2 am and 2 pm it is busy with the release of glycogen from the liver. At the same time, in the liver there is a counter-rhythm involving a slow increase in bile production from 2 am, which reaches its peak level around 2 pm and then again slowly decreases to its lowest level around 2 am.

The release of glycogen between 2 am and 2 pm means that the liver is in a depletion phase during this period. The body releases its energy reserves, gained during the regenerative nighttime hours, throughout the morning so that consciousness, which is maintained through the utilization of blood sugar, is available for learning and development through age-appropriate activities. This is a physical depletion process which leads to the deposit and formation of nerve substance. This formation process is put on hold during the midday slump when the processes of nourishing and secreting step into the foreground and the "I" is mainly concentrated in the area of the torso. One could also put it this way: Compared to a person's capability of perception in the morning, in the early afternoon one is not able to utilize the blood as much for thinking (and, in the first seven-year period, not as much for sensory perceptions) because it is circulating more through other areas of the body at this time. It is a fact that the temperature of the limbs is lower in the early afternoon (Gelitz, 2009). As soon as the nourishing process recedes into the background during the course of the afternoon, physiological performance capability increases again and paves the way for the second period of high performance capability of the day. However, now the "readiness for depletion" in the liver and gallbladder is lower and is not increasing as it does during the morning hours; glycogen reserves are being built up again as bile production steadily decreases. Therefore one can speak here of a high point in performance level that offers less of a possibility for strengthening nerve connections and much more of a possibility for unconscious limb-system activity.

Processes of depletion and breaking down always indicate chances for realization and formation (or rather, learning), whereas processes of building up and construction always indicate the possibility of deliberate activity in the unconscious.

In children of kindergarten age there are less noticeable differences in this regard because the only differences possible are in the time of day chosen for different activities. However, in school-age children one notices a clear difference between an intellectual high point reached in the morning and a physical (sports, music) high point reached in the afternoon.

As Steiner described in *The Spiritual Guidance of the Individual and Humanity* (GA 15), "It must certainly be taken into consideration that everything that is referred to as training or lessons for the intellect should be undertaken with children in the morning hours. Only after this has been accomplished will the children be led into the more physically-oriented activities in the afternoon; that is, if they have not already let off a lot of steam during the morning recess. And after these physical education activities have taken place, the children will not be brought back into the classroom for more intellectual activity. I have already indicated that such a thing has a destructive effect on life…"

Thus, the school day is structured in a healthy way when subjects like mathematics, physics, and foreign languages are taught before the midday slump, in accordance with physical-etheric requirements. Then, after a long break, during which the body is able to concentrate on digesting lunch — without any energy demands for intellectual pursuits — is a good time to schedule such things as physical education and sports, handicrafts, painting and drawing, a hiking group, etc. With homework, one should take care that the children begin it in the late afternoon, because they are able to perform at a peak level at that time of day.

How is it possible for the individual subjects, such as arithmetic, writing, and foreign language, to breathe? First of all, one has to create a bridge from that which has been to what will be in the future. It is healthy when students have to remember at the beginning of a class; that is, when they can gently breathe into what was before and, after a link has been established, they are able to devote themselves entirely to the new material; and the conclusion of the lesson should include a preview of the next class. In this way there is not a permanent, high demand for concentration, but rather one of increasing demand for concentration, followed by a steady demand and concluding with decreasing demand.

Secondly, the lessons are permeated with a breathing quality by having a healthy alternation between receiving and active doing; that is, between forming thoughts and concepts through listening, and active participation in the form of painting, writing, clapping, singing, running, and so on.

The tempo of speech or the speed in which successive thoughts and concepts are artfully introduced is another way for superimposed rhythms to pulse through the lessons. In this way the more taxing parts of the lesson can be alternated with "easier" parts, which makes for a healthy, "breathing" lesson for children as well as teachers.

Knowledge of chronobiology can help get us on the right track in regard to configuring the school day and class schedule so that they have a breathing quality. This special branch of science, the "biology of time," has steadily gained importance in the last twenty years and has also found its way into mainstream publications, outside of scientific journals. Life is organized according to rhythms anchored in the physical-etheric (bio-rhythms), but there are certain conditions in the human organism that are only marginally changeable and this is where the unstable balance between health and illness becomes apparent. Chronobiologists study variances in performance abilities during the day, differences in body temperature over a 24-hour period, changes in the release of hormones, reaction times and many other things. The more this knowledge is incorporated into our educational structures, the healthier our schools can become.

The breathing life process has taken up comparatively more space in this chapter than the other life processes, because this realm belongs everything that has to do with rhythm, including the daily schedule and the flow of activity within each lesson. The following pages will more briefly address each of the other life processes. As we have said before, what is written here will hopefully provide an impulse in the reader for further observation.

When we turn our attention to the *warming* life process, the first questions that come to mind are: Is my teaching interesting? Do I spark enthusiasm in the children? Am I, myself, interested and enthusiastic? It has to do with

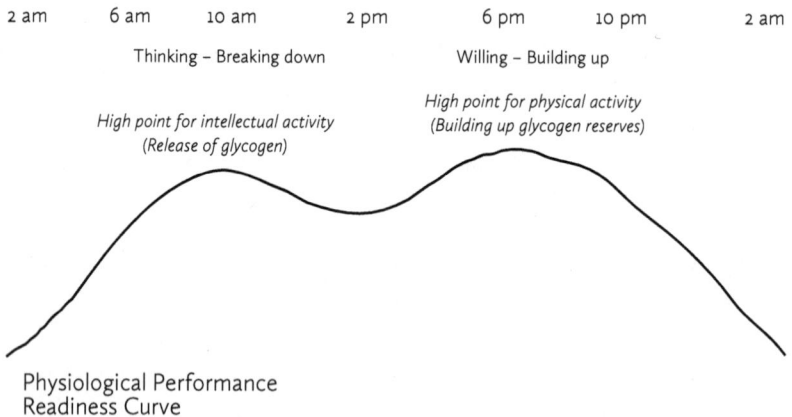

FIGURE 17
Performance readiness and
the liver-gallbladder rhythm.

cultivating the soul faculties of interest and enthusiasm, which have developed from out of the warmth production life process, and allowing them to unfold. That is to say, the first thing to strive for is that every lesson sparks enthusiasm! The best way to accomplish this is with imaginative and artistic teaching, paired with the possibility of the children doing some activities themselves. This is warming for children, in body and soul.

But there is something else that is necessary. Besides providing warmth for the body and sparking enthusiasm in the soul, "warming" also means entering into a healthy relationship with the external world. On a hot summer's day the physical organism has to be able to cool the body, otherwise there would be over-heating and fever. The ability to adapt, which is available to a child as a soul faculty beginning in the first school years, has to be further cultivated as well. Consideration, empathy, patience, and the desire to help — these are all attributes that are able to develop from out of soul adaptability. Therefore, a child's social competence is also a question of cultivating the ability to adapt and conform to the external (social) environment. In this way, engagement with the warming life process in school-age children could become a persuasive argument in favor of having classes made up of children with varying capacities, as is the case in most Waldorf schools. Creating integrated, or inclusive, classes in which children with and without special challenges learn together, represents great progress from this standpoint.

However, it is not only the students who have to learn to socially adapt but also the teachers, who have the responsibility of presenting the material to be learned at a "soul temperature" which will enable children to join in with interest and enthusiasm. It is of no use to a fourth-grader if an enthusiastic mathematics teacher gives an impassioned speech about the origin of fractions. What children need much more is an adult who prepares them for the subject in such a way that they are able to become enthusiastic about it. In other words, it has to be understandable and manageable in order to arouse interest.

Regarding the *nourishing* life process as it relates to school: Everything should be arranged in such a way that nothing stands in the way of inner connections, of the soul being able to receive. Anchoring of the nourishing processes in the physical body is what produces the soul faculties of receiving, making inner connections, and breaking down and analyzing. How are we able to cultivate this?

Some examples are: providing real soul nourishment in the form of fairy tales, fables, legends, or other meaningful stories; making sure the "appetizers" in the form of material to be learned are not too large; seeing to it that "hard to digest" material can be "precooked" by "providing a foretaste"; or perhaps by really getting down to the nitty-gritty with some topic (that is, splitting it apart and breaking it down into smaller components for analysis).

If problems arise, it could be that the nourishing life process is not anchored well enough in the physical body and therefore the corresponding soul faculties have been inadequately released. Then it may be necessary for parents and teachers to discuss questions of nutrition and of demonstrating "nourishing" work processes, such as cooking, which are worthy of imitation.

If a child is presented with gentle nourishment for the soul that contains real and true pictures and digestible subject matter, then she is in a position to maintain and increase her ability to receive, while too much challenge would have a slowly crippling effect and could even encourage a tendency to illness. Something that belongs in the "too demanding" category is speech that is too abstract. Who has not caught themselves every now and then speaking to children in a cool, intellectual manner? For instance, there are many possibilities when it comes to answering questions like: Why is the Moon sometimes shaped like a crescent and sometimes like a circle and sometimes you can't see it at all? The more an adult's imagination is engaged, the better a child is able to accept a given answer, without "poisoning" the child:

> Intellectual wisdom is, in fact, a kind of poison as soon as it lands in the wrong place; as soon, at least, as it gets into the metabolic system. We are only able to live with intellectual wisdom if this poison — I say this completely in a technical sense and not with any kind of moral judgment — does not penetrate down into our metabolic-limb system. It has a terribly destructive effect there. But with children this stiffness and hardness is not present. If we approach them with our mature wisdom of today, this poison does indeed penetrate down into the metabolic-limb system and poisons it. You see, it is important to learn to know directly from life just how much can be expected from these children's heads so that one does not try to fill them with more than they can hold causing it to go down into the metabolic-limb system. As a teacher and artist of education, you have within your grasp the power to affect a child's organism either in a health-promoting or health-destroying way (Steiner, The Spiritual Guidance of the Individual and Humanity, GA 15).

On the topic of secreting, it should be noted that for school children it is a benevolent act if the content of a subject (tempered by age-appropriateness) is divided up in proportion to the abundance of the material to be learned. Then children will not be over-challenged, even if faced with complicated references of logic, but rather their capacity for sorting and organizing will be challenged and strengthened. If the demonstration of formulas does not take precedence it will lead to a deep sense of satisfaction because a mixture of experiences can then be incorporated into a logical whole.

One example of this would be writing out number series during arithmetic class in the lower grades. Before anything is written, the numbers are first clapped, jumped, and sung; in this way they are internalized in a form that is divided and manageable. From ages seven or eight, something like this has become a pressing need of the soul, just as it is a physical necessity to sort food substances in the stomach and intestines into what is needed and what is to be eliminated. Once the children are older, the sorting and ordering capacity is applied to the aspect of time. For instance, children are especially encouraged in their sorting abilities if a painting or piece of music is brought into its historical context during art or music classes. This is a sensible way of cultivating the soul faculty of sorting and organizing, much better than handing out photocopies of cold formulas and diagrams.

The less a child is capable of internal sorting and organization, the more it will be necessary to focus again on imitating external ordering processes. Having an organized backpack and neat and orderly main lesson books are very practical helps; but also maintaining order and organization in the entire class during play, physical education, and eurythmy.

In regard to the *maintaining* life process and the soul faculty of memory that comes out of it, it is very important to structure enough space for remembering. Also how freely the memory is able to develop depends in large part upon the quality of questions asked. Naturally, the most important factor is having enough time for all the students to follow along when delving into the past, even those students who achieve conceptual and associative thinking more slowly. Another important factor is the expansiveness of the space created. If a question about something in the past is too diffuse or lacks specificity, no answers will be forthcoming because a point of reference is missing. On the other hand, if a question is too specific, then a child will have too little experience to call upon in order to come up with an answer.

Additionally, if there are problems in school having to do with the faculty of memory, this can be resolved by turning once again to an external process of maintaining, which will support the anchoring of the maintaining life process resulting in the release of the soul faculty of memory. Some examples in the space of a classroom would be cleaning the blackboard, returning the eraser to its place, and pushing the chairs back under the table. An example for the time aspect would be reciting the morning verse in the familiar, recognizable fashion, but with a stronger emphasis on gestures. A repeated gesture provides an impulse for the activity of remembering without over-challenging the ability to pull something from out of the head at will, an ability that may be inadequately developed under certain circumstances.

In regard to the *growing* life process in school, the magic word is: Practice! Nothing allows for the development of the freshly-born soul faculties of inner growth, expansion, and the possibility of improvement better than continuous repetition and practice.

Engaging children's metabolic-limb pole through active participation means having them always do the same, or similar, things. Some things that are especially well-suited for practice in the first grade, for example, are form drawing, recitation, singing, and recurrent games. Engaging children's life of thought and imagination — the nerve-sense pole — means allowing children to repeatedly penetrate with their thinking something that has just happened. For instance, reviewing a main lesson block that has just ended or repeating a main lesson block at the end of the school year allows children to experience their own growth. The time of growth and maturing is made apparent in the repetition — that is, of course, if the exact same material is not merely monotonously repeated. There should be endless variations that make the material always seem fresh and new.

The *reproducing* life process involves cultivating children's ability to form their own ideas. Yesterday, the sunset seemed redder than usual. Does anyone have an idea about that? How can it be that the stars twinkle? This soul faculty stems from the reproducing process and is gradually released and becomes autonomous through the physical process of producing – reproducing.

Besides such questions as those above, which cultivate opportunities for development of ideas, anything that leads children to create something completely new is very stimulating: art and handwork classes, for example, as long as they leave the children free enough to create something of their own. Composing little songs, painting pictures, carving candlesticks, or sewing one's own pencil case are all opportunities for cultivating the gradually released faculties from the producing – reproducing processes. Also belonging to this realm is respect for the rules that children come up with for games. If adults do not interfere with children's own rules for social games, games that improve motor skills, or sports, they have the opportunity to practice the development of ideas in a very strong way.

Within the realm of the producing – reproducing life processes, everything having to do with creating and producing something oneself is healthy and beneficial, whether through thinking, art, or handwork.

The following could be considered in schools: The flow and sequence of lessons could actually be structured in such a way that at the beginning of the class there is inhalation. How are you? What is the weather like today? What happened yesterday? This allows children to warm up to the subject matter; interest in going further is awakened and the adult brings the subject to an age-appropriate "soul temperature." If this is successful, creation of an inner connection is possible; first, by way of language filled with imagery and second, by way of active participation by the students. Then things can be sorted out during class discussions: What belongs where? How is one thing connected to the other? What is not important? Now the discussion can take a turn toward maintaining and preserving: How was that again? Does it have something to do with yesterday? And then it can be expanded, with practice and striving for improvement taking their place in the structure of the lesson: writing practice, doing arithmetic, singing the same song several times, etc. The conclusion of the class could include encouragement for developing one's own ideas, perhaps in the form of writing a poem, composing music, or painting a picture — or maybe a stimulating question will come up during the course of the day.

The more teachers occupy themselves with these questions and have discussions together about them, putting aside any banal, well-worn phrases about a rhythmic daily schedule, the healthier a school can become.

It is also important to mention that cultivating the released soul faculties has a reciprocal effect on the physical aspect of the seven life processes. This is most clearly shown, from practical life experience, using the example of warmth production. When children (and also adults) are interested and enthusiastic about something they become warm. Healthy blood circulation depends upon whether or not a specific subject is prepared at the right level and temperature so that the blood alters its movements by way of interest and enthusiasm. The same applies to the other life processes. If children are properly awakened to perception and attentiveness it brings about healthy breathing. If children are rightly brought to making inner connections, to sorting and keeping things separate, this has a healthy effect on metabolism. Last but not least, children also grow because they practice. There are reciprocal effects and interdependencies between the physical and soul aspects of the seven life processes. For a healthy school it is extremely important to pay attention to this fact if we do not wish to make the children pale and ill through our teaching.

Finally, the topic of schools and the seven life processes should also include the question of what kind of influence the upheaval and agitation of puberty, the birth of the astral body, has on the released soul faculties as a result of the effects of the seven life processes. In connection with the nourishing life process, the faculty of skeptical dismantling and deconstruction has already been discussed. In connection with the secreting life process, the faculty of critical analysis, which joins with the ability to bring things in order, was identified. Regarding the producing – reproducing life process, we explained that this process is associated with the formation of one's own ideas and with discovering ideals — that is, with the development of great social ideas and ideals.

Education toward freedom is the basic goal of Waldorf education, in that, above all, it has to do with uncovering "that which wants to be born." This always involves structuring an environment in which adults are included. For an organization based on freedom and personal responsibility, it is necessary to allow for the possibility of individual development. If it is not possible to call into question that which already exists, or if early childhood education is conceived on the basis of utility, then the past will repeat itself, new impulses will not be born, and the forces of health will be permanently under assault. Whether a society can be carried by its members, or only endured, depends upon the educational system: "The question should not be: 'What kind of knowledge and abilities does a person need in order to be useful to the social order?' Rather, the question should be: 'What dispositions are already present in a person and what can be developed in him?' " (Steiner, GA 24). It is a question of whether or not a person is able to achieve independence; growing up means growing out of the existing norms and pre-conceived notions of the parents in order to develop post-conventional morality and moral imagination. In this way a need for democracy arises, rather than a need to be guided and managed.

When an individual steps onto the world stage and his or her own actions, feeling life, and judgments are no longer dependent upon the authority of parents and teachers, there is a deepening of soul experience. That is to say, a young person is then able to not only concentrate with devoted attention, but is also able to search the world for the object of his concentration. He is not only able to warm to something with interest and enthusiasm, but can also draw on the consequences of his enthusiasm and produce warmth in his surroundings through words and actions. He can not only maintain and preserve his own self, but is also able to preserve the world. And, he can not only practice and improve, but can also motivate himself to be occupied with specific subjects and activities.

After puberty, new soul-spiritual faculties appear:

Perception of the world – Global thinking

Enthusiasm for the surroundings – Rhetoric

Deconstruction of the world – Skepticism

Ordering of connected things – Analysis

Consequential action – Preserving values

Inner activity – Stringency

Forming social ideas – Discovering ideals

Acquiring these faculties is the goal of the upper school curriculum; the world can now be recognized as something whole and connected, which is the foundation for developing a holistic world view. However, the faculties will only be engaged if the life processes, and the first soul faculties to come out of them, are cultivated in the home, kindergarten, and school. Without global, or holistic, thinking; without the ability to persuade through rhetoric; skepticism; without the ability to separate and analyze; without a certain conservation of values; without stringency in internal and external activities; and idealism — without all these things it will be difficult to stand in the world if one wishes to act out of one's own judgment and does not wish to be at the mercy of authority and current fashions. The importance for later life of nurturing and cultivating the seven life processes in kindergarten and the beginning school years is, once again, made abundantly clear.

The Seven Life Processes as a Concrete View of the Etheric

If we could gaze down at our blue planet like the astronauts, we would probably get a better idea of the Earth's atmosphere than we are able to using only our power of imagination. Life is possible only within this atmosphere. The four elements work together within it to form the most varied bodies and life forms, always in conjunction with forces which Rudolf Steiner called "formative forces" or "etheric forces": as he said in *Illness and Therapy* (GA 313), "Etheric forces are always polar-opposite to the forces working in physical matter."

He clearly distinguished between the formative forces, which are to be understood as the builders of the physical body, and the four ethers that work in our atmosphere and in our physical body as well. Just as matter and elements must combine to form substances, so, in turn, the substances, combined with the ethers, have to be formed by way of the formative forces. Steiner differentiated between warmth ether, light ether, chemical ether, and life ether. Further research into this thought process alone could fill a lifetime. How can we get nearer to an understanding of life through the attempt to connect natural science with spiritual science and our wakeful, questioning observations?

We would like to point out that we are not posing this question only as it relates to anthroposophy. The question highlights the fact that anyone seeking understanding of human beings is confronted with this idea: "Everything visible originates in the invisible" (Lommel, 2011).

Today, science has arrived at this thought. Through the discoveries of quantum physics and the concepts of non-space and non-time, along with discoveries about elementary particles, which seem to be ever-shrinking in size (protons, neutrons, quarks, and now even the Higgs boson particles), the age-old question of how physical matter is created is being researched.

"The visible, material world of space and time is a complement to the invisible, imperceptible, non-local space... Already...Newton took into consideration the fact that omnipresent space could be filled with spiritual substance" (Lommel, 2011).

In the meantime, this search for matter and anti-matter connects natural science with spiritual science. Amazing self-healing processes (Kuby, 2005) or experiences with nourishment from light (Werner and Stöckli, 2012) bring up questions that require a new openness. Current scientific research on the light-nourishment process illustrates the advanced views which Rudolf Steiner described in detail in *The Agriculture Course* (GA 327) in 1924. The long silence about these research results illustrates the fear and insecurity surrounding questions of spirituality and hidden things. The extent to which science must change is becoming clear.

The thought that our understanding must be expanded to include ideas such as energy fields, resonance, chi, and so on has already been accepted in many places. The quantum physicist David Bohm (1917–92) described an implicit organization of being as a fundamental, higher-dimensional information field based on holographic principles. Without any measureable transfer of energy, "in-formation" is produced, a form-giving principle (See Lommel, 2011). The physicist Henry Stapp postulated in 2004 that scientists who searched only for references to physical matter were hindering the progress of science. With anthroposophy we are able to *use natural science as the basis* to go beyond purely material references and learn to understand the world holistically.

In the previous chapters we have attempted to present the seven life processes individually and to illustrate the importance of nurturing them in education. In the following section we will focus on understanding the etheric, the living basis for our earthly existence, and, once again, deepening our understanding from an anthroposophical point of view. This will give us the opportunity to make a little progress "on the trail of living substances." As was already mentioned at the beginning, there are many facets of the etheric that would serve well for gaining understanding of living substances, but here we will turn our gaze toward the seven life processes. However, since these always pervade the many other vantage points from which one is able to view living organisms, we will give two brief examples of the interplay between various levels.

One example is the human being in earthly form, which is seen as being placed into the world as a three-fold organism. The human being displays three different systems of function:

The nerve-sense system, located mainly in the head, has to do with everything related to sensory organs and nerve systems and their synthesis in the brain; it forms the basis of the life of concepts and imagination in the soul and waking consciousness in the spirit.

The rhythmic system, located mainly in the chest region, has to do with everything related to breathing, blood circulation and physical rhythms; it forms the basis of the life of feeling in the soul and dream consciousness in the spirit.

The metabolic-limb system, located mainly in limb movement and the area of substance transformation, that is, the digestive tract, but also in the release of warmth resulting from muscle movement. The soul uses it as a basis for the will, action, and activity, and it also forms the basis for sleeping consciousness in the spirit.

These three intermingled but functionally separate systems in the human organism are all permeated by the seven life processes. Within a differentiated view of child development, one is able to observe how the release of life forces occurs in three stages. A look at the seven life processes also highlights this threefold aspect. We see that a child does not suddenly awaken out of the physical body at age six or seven with the ability to perceive, become interested in things, or concentrate on things. Naturally, a child is able to perceive things right after birth, but is not yet able to organize them or understand what is being perceived.

If the nerve-sense system has reached a certain level of development at around age two-and-a-half with myelinization (covering of the neural pathways), one is able to determine by a child's ability to formulate questions that the secreting life process has partially dissolved itself out of the nerve formation process. Likewise, during this time we find a change in breathing, which, from now on, becomes diaphragm breathing, along with an awakening to the self; a child says "I." However, asking questions does not mean that a child has need of abstract, cognitive answers. The nerve-sense system structure first has to continue forming the instrument of the brain until the frontal lobes are connected and abstract thinking can be brought into action.

If the rhythmic system, at just about five years old, has continued to develop with growth in the lungs and lowering of the costal margin (lower edge of ribs), then an increasing capability of attentiveness is produced. Now, a child not "only" perceives, but is able to attentively look and listen. There is no more fidgeting of the legs while listening to a story and a child is able to receive what is being said close by. The structuring, formative forces gradually free themselves from the rhythmic system.

If the metabolic-limb system has achieved a certain level of development around age seven, one can observe that a child will decide to practice something and then be able to carry out the intention. The limbs have become so skillful that the metabolism no longer influences their behavior so strongly, and a child has the will and ability to put thoughts into action.

The danger is that the release of these emerging faculties is misused by usurping these forces for adult-style, intellectual learning, thereby hindering the process of healthy development. A three-year-old's faculty of perception or joy in asking questions, and the attentiveness of a five-year-old, must not be too heavily challenged; life forces are still needed for the transformation of the metabolic-limb system.

There would be no sense organs or nerves if all seven life processes did not maintain them; no dynamic, rhythmic center of a human being in the chest cavity, with breathing, pulse, peristaltic, and changeable rhythms, without the seven life processes making them possible in the first place; and no metabolic organs and processes, no bones in the limbs, and no muscle activity without the constant pulsing of the seven life processes.

If it can be said that the etheric body protects physical conditions in the human body from decay, then the only reason it is able to achieve this is because of the seven life processes living within it. If we were to take away even one of the life processes, human life would be impossible! The seven life processes also form the basic physical preconditions for the threefold nature of the human soul in the form of thinking, feeling, and willing.

Something similar can be said for the four different areas of the sensory world, the four elements, and for the four different areas of the etheric, the so-called four ethers. The seven life processes also play into this second example; the areas of the four elements and the four ethers. Through the process of Earth's development, four elemental conditions appeared; warmth, air (gaseous), watery or liquid, and earthy (solid). The etheric counter-images of these four elements are called the four ethers; warmth ether, light ether, chemical (or tone) ether, and life ether. (An especially comprehensive and detailed work on the four ethers and how they relate to the four elements can be found in Ernst Marti's book, *The Four Ethers*.) All of these four areas of the etheric and physical are permeated by the seven life processes.

These four areas are very apparent in common plants like flowers or trees. The *life ether* allows the plant to become a life form. When a seed is surrounded by the elements, the life ether stirs something in the seed which allows the tender roots to be able to connect with the solid earth and absorb minerals from it, forming a living connection. Because of the life ether, a plant, as a physical formation consisting of carbon, hydrogen, nitrogen, oxygen, etc., is able to be perceived by the senses. The workings of the life ether bring about an integrated whole in the physical, material realm.

On the one hand, the *chemical ether* (or *tone ether*) allows plants to become life forms with a fluid distribution system in which the laws of levity and buoyancy can prevail. Through this area of the etheric, fluid is brought into the outermost peripheries. On the other hand, this is the area of the etheric which makes it possible for plants to even have chemistry in the first place; meaning there are not simply random substances present, but rather previously non-existent chemical compounds, fats, proteins, carbohydrates and gases. This is the area of the etheric which allows the most varied wonders of form to appear by way of formative forces which separate and join physical, material substances.

Light ether gives plants the possibility of unfolding and developing in air and light. Through this force, with the presence of both air and light, photosynthesis — the "reversed breathing" of plants — and production of chlorophyll are possible. It lifts the plant's chemistry up to higher level, now dependent upon air and light. Flowers, the airiest and most gorgeously hued manifestation of plants, along with their radiating, symmetrical shapes, are also the results of the workings of light ether. They draw a life form into the spatial aspect.

Warmth ether is the area of living elements through which a plant shows itself to be a being of warmth — that is, a living structure that releases warmth even in its earliest stages. However, a plant does not produce warmth within itself, but only absorbs warmth and then allows it to work throughout its organism. This can be observed with sugar production in fruit. The more a plant is exposed to the sun, the sweeter its fruit. It is not only a question of light, but also of warmth. These areas of the etheric make it possible for a life form to develop and mature within time.

All four of these ethers and the conditions of existence related to them (elements) are either touched or permeated by the seven life processes. Without the life processes no mineral-solvent roots, watery stems, airy leaves, or sugary fruits could survive; the difference is that in plants the seven life processes are less internal than they are in human beings and animals.

Additionally, in humans and animals the solid (earth) element is found in bones and nerves, the fluid (water) element in the lymphatic system, interstitial fluid, blood, etc., the air element through taking in air and gaseous formations from air, and the warmth (fire) element in the development of warmth and its distribution by way of the bloodstream. Humans and animals are also material entities which can be perceived by the senses (life ether), are beings possessing internal chemistry, capable of separating and combining substances (chemical ether), as well as radially symmetric organisms which grow in air and light (light ether) and develop and mature over time (warmth ether) (Marti, 1984).

So, as living beings, humans and animals also have the four ethers within themselves, without which the four elements would not be able to appear at a physical-sensory level.

The previously described four areas of the ethers in plants are all touched by the seven life processes, but with animals and humans — the more highly developed life forms — the seven life processes permeate them through and through; they pulse and flow through everything that is solid, liquid, airy, and warm. There would be no hardening in bones and nerves, no chemical processes in organs and cells, no living, air-filled cavities and no warmth without the seven life processes. With this, we are thrust into the matter of the anthroposophical aspect of the seven life processes: What do the seven life processes look like in plants, animals, and human beings? What are the differences? What influence does the astral body (and in humans, the "I") have on the development of the seven life processes? These questions should be addressed at least on a basic level in order to come to a somewhat more detailed view of the etheric.

Plants, Animals, and Human Beings

Plants, animals, and human beings are all organisms in which the conditions of the four elements appear: solid, liquid, air and warmth. On the most basic level, they have this in common. The conditions of the four elements are apparent in all living things because they possess an etheric body.

The first thing to be observed in plants is that they combine the same life processes as animals and humans, except that in plants the life processes are not so internalized. The seven life processes *touch* plants more from the outside; with plants it is more a matter of *turning to* the life processes rather than taking them in.

Thus, the *breathing* of plants does not take place in an internal organ like the lungs in more highly developed animals and humans; it takes place on the periphery. The process of taking in carbon dioxide, producing chlorophyll, and giving off oxygen happens on leaf surfaces.

Warming is also a very external process. Plants do not maintain constant "body warmth" but are more like the hematocryal (cold-blooded) lower animals like fish, reptiles, amphibians, and insects; they are approximately as warm as the environment. In spite of this, plants are *touched* by the warmth production life process, in that they need a temperature range which allows them to survive. Furthermore, with plants there is always a certain amount of temperature regulation of the environment going on because of their system of fluid distribution. In summer a forest is cooler than an adjacent meadow, and in winter the snow closest to trees melts quicker because a slightly warmer microclimate has been created there.

With regard to *nourishing*, plants nourish themselves more directly and produce no organ-based metabolic activity. Plants are nourished with the needed mineral substances and correct amount of water through their roots and are likewise directly nourished through their leaf surfaces with carbon dioxide, a carbon bond. This process allows carbohydrates, proteins, and sugars to form but it does not demolish them in an internal digestive tract as happens in animals and humans. Plants merely take in substances; they do not demolish living substances.

This also brings up the question of *secreting*. Plants do not take in more than they need for their development and therefore do not possess organs of elimination. Substances which are no longer needed are directly expended through the respiration of the leaves and, during the course of a plant's growth, parts are always dying off and falling, such as wilted leaves or rotten branches.

In plants, *maintaining* is also not a regeneration process guided by organs. It is much more readily explained by the very nature of plants; they maintain and regenerate themselves by growing and allowing old parts to wilt. That is to say, they have a flexibility that preserves them from breakage. The power of human beings and many animals to heal a wound has been much less internalized by plants. Certainly, damage to a stalk, stem or bark can be held in check or even "healed" by covering with sap. But even so, germs in the form of mold spores and bacteria infect the wound immediately and cause great harm to the plant. They do not have any organ-based immunity against pathogens. Someone has to seal a wound on a tree in order to prevent disease, performing the healing function for the plant from the outside.

It is interesting to look at the *growing* life process in plants; they possess this process in a very remarkable way that is different from humans and animals. First, a plant's growth is much more dependent on the surroundings — on light and warmth — and second, a plant changes its form very significantly during the course of its growth. This change in form is many, many times less in human beings and animals. The only times it is that noticeable is during prenatal development in the womb or egg, or in the transformation from larva to insect. Aside from comparatively few changes in proportions, the form of an animal or human being stays the same after birth or hatching. In contrast, a plant changes its form to a remarkable degree. Just compare a sunflower shortly after germination with the stage of leaf development and finally when it is in full bloom; it is hardly recognizable from one stage to the next. Or, compare an oak tree in the first two years of growth and then again after 100 years! One is able to gain an idea of how soul faculties that come out of the astral sphere are internalized in animals and humans, leading to physical organ formation. The growing life process is much more strongly connected to physical inner life in animals and humans than it is in plants, which gravitate towards air and light and insects in the surroundings, toward that which is influenced by the astral — they have not internalized it. In contrast, human beings and animals have already internalized these influences and carry them within their own physical organisms. However, since prenatal development is just as rapid as the transformation of physical form that takes place in plants, it should be noted here that the internalization of soul aspects in humans and animals is only possible with the maturing of internal organs. An animal or human fetus strives toward the astral with rapidly changing growth, just like a plant, until the physical basis for internalization of the astral has been created. After that, human beings and animals maintain their recognizable forms. Therefore, pure etheric life is a continuous metamorphosis which is first restrained by the soul and spirit.

With *reproducing* we again see that a plant has not internalized this life process to a high degree. Plants do indeed create their fruits or seeds, but not from out of themselves and definitely not from any act of procreation. Seed formation in plants does not happen "just like that," but rather because they stand in the middle of the surrounding nature. Certainly, human beings and animals are also dependent upon outside influences when it comes to procreation, but not to the same degree as plants. Plants stretch toward air, light, and warmth, and most are dependent upon the help of insects for pollination to occur. For instance, the ripening of seed kernels into fruit is dependent upon the sun. Later, mature seeds are often dependent upon the wind or birds so that they fall on fertile ground. In this regard, it is especially interesting to note that plants can in no way bring about pollination by themselves. All that is played out in the plant world is simply the production of seeds which are subsequently pollinated by "Mother" Earth (Steiner, *Harmony of the Creative Word*, GA 230). Any kind of sexual development is missing in plants. Male plants are the only kinds that exist!

Another kind of production process already mentioned is the production of chlorophyll, which is connected with leaf respiration. This also does not take place in an internal organ system, but happens when the necessary conditions prevail in the exact place they are needed. Human beings produce red blood cells in the bone marrow (or in the liver as embryos), and coagulant proteins in the liver — not in a thousand other places, wherever blood circulates. In contrast, plants produce chlorophyll in every single cell separately. Looking at this from a phenomenological perspective, we are able to recognize three things:

First: Plants turn to the seven life processes without having internalized them. They touch the sphere of the seven life processes without living *in* them, but are rather much more *surrounded* by them.

Second: Internalization of the seven life processes in human beings and animals has to do with the astrality that lives within them; in this they are the opposite of plants. An organism *without* an astral body *turns to* the seven life processes. An organism *with* an astral body has the seven life processes *within it*. It is clear that the seven life processes are an etheric principle that can only exist through the influence of an astral sphere. The astral influences the form of being of the etheric; or seen from the other side, the form of being of the etheric, with seven processes flowing through it, facilitates the astral.

Third: Physical organs are astral formations. Only perceptive, soul-bearing beings carry within them internal organs, sensory organs, nerves, muscles, etc. They become physical "enabling organs" for sensory perception and movement in animals and human beings; additionally, in human beings they are places where cognizance, feelings, and will-driven actions are enabled. Plants do not have any of this. A plant is a "pure" etheric-physical being without an internalized astral influence.

We do find the aforementioned organs in animals. They have internal organs, sensory organs, nerves, and a movement apparatus. The previously described internalization of the seven life processes through the presence of the astral in the physical organism is easily studied here. In the animal kingdom we are dealing with *organ-based* processes and not with external breathing, nourishing, or reproducing processes.

The connection between the astral and the anchoring of the seven life processes in the physical organs becomes very clear in the variety of ways individual animal species have developed. The less-developed animals, which have taken in less astrality, exhibit less, or more rudimentary, anchoring of the life processes in their organisms than the more highly developed mammals which, like human beings, carry the life processes completely internally and are therefore better able to move around in the world, independent of external influences.

Here, we would like to mention a few examples of differences within the animal kingdom. *Fish*, for example, with their gills, exhibit a breathing process that extends further into the organism than is the case with plants.

Furthermore, they of course take oxygen from the water and not carbon dioxide like plants. That being said, it is a breathing process that does not lead deep into the inner regions of the body as is the case with lungs in other animals. Besides, fish are cold-blooded animals, meaning their body temperature is dependent upon the surrounding water temperature. The warming life process is not yet so internalized that it is possible to maintain a constant body temperature. However, fish certainly do seek out areas where the water temperature is comfortable for them. Reproduction in fish is still an external process in which the spawn thrive outside of the mother-organism. Sometimes special places must be found which offer optimal conditions for hatching fish. Other reproduction processes are internalized, such as blood, organ, or muscle formation. The nourishing, secreting and maintaining life processes also proceed in the internal organism.

The next animal group to consider is *reptiles*. There is a big difference between fish on the one hand and turtles, lizards, and snakes on the other: Reptiles use lungs for breathing. For this reason the breathing life process is more strongly anchored. Even though with animals one cannot speak of a release of physically-bound life processes to be used for soul faculties, there is still a difference in the "focused" movement and gaze of reptiles as compared to fish. Stronger internalization of breathing leads to a somewhat different, more directed approach to the world. Stronger internalization of the astral, and the finer sensitivity and power of soul expression associated with it, correlates with internalization of the life processes. This is a further example of the influence of the astral on the etheric constitution of human beings and animals.

However, reptiles, like fish, cannot produce their own warmth. They are also cold-blooded animals in which the intensity of life functions, such as their pulse, is dependent upon the external temperature. With these animals all activity is reduced and becomes slower in cold temperatures, from heartbeat to food intake to movement. Furthermore, reptiles also lay eggs like fish, so the life process of reproducing takes place outside the physical organism, at least partially.

In regard to breathing, *amphibians*, like salamanders or frogs, but also *insects* and spiders, stand somewhere between fish and reptiles. Insects breathe using trachea, which are small, branch-like tubes located on the periphery of the body; they are not lungs. Some amphibians have gills and lungs and some can even breathe very substantially through the skin. With regard to anchoring of the life processes, it is interesting to note that honeybees can raise the temperature of the hive in relation to external temperatures by collective muscle twitching. To be sure, they are also cold-blooded animals, but they can at least produce some warmth using their own energy.

Like reptiles, birds have lungs with which they have internalized the breathing life process. What puts them a stage higher than reptiles is their constant body temperature. Birds maintain a warm body temperature, at least in the torso. They have internalized the warming life process to a large extent. Since the life processes influence each other, this also affects the stability of the breathing processes in birds. With cold-blooded reptiles, breathing, heart rate, and movement all slow down and there is reduced food intake whenever external temperatures are cold. This is not the case with birds. Because of the constant temperature in a bird's body all the life functions and movement are able to constantly take place. That is why a sparrow does not hop or fly any faster in summer than in winter. In contrast, fish, reptiles, amphibians, and insects become slower with increasing cold.

However, birds have not yet completely internalized the reproducing process. They lay eggs, and for this reason part of the reproducing process takes place outside of their organism, although their own body warmth is needed. Because birds incubate their eggs through brooding, they exhibit a stronger connection with this external reproducing process than is the case with fish, frogs, turtles, and flies. Without brooding no chicks or fledglings could develop; constant warmth is necessary for the survival of chicks not yet hatched.

Finally, *mammals* have all seven life processes internally anchored just like human beings. Not only do they have lungs, a constant body temperature, and internalized metabolic activity, they also have reproduction of offspring inside the mother's body. Developing offspring in the mother requires a womb, formation of the amniotic sac, amniotic fluid, and placenta, and birth of a "finished" organism through the birth canal. The newborn must also drink mother's milk after birth.

The seven life processes are similarly anchored in mammals and human beings. They both have taken in a high amount of astrality. They are alert, endowed with senses, find joy in movement, and have no vital functions that take place outside their own organism. This shows how the anchoring of the seven life processes in the internal organism is connected with the astrality that is taken into the organism.

The etheric body of an animal, as opposed to that of a plant, is changed through astrality because the etheric must now follow the determinations of the astral. In animals the life functions do not stand alone but rather serve biological instincts, drives, and desires. Plants are not influenced in this way, and animals, as will be shown, are influenced by the astral, in ways that differ depending upon the stage of development.

Now, it is true that the life functions in human beings are also under the influence of soul-astral instincts, drives, and desires, but not exclusively. They additionally serve a motive. A human being possesses an ego ("I") that motivates actions, can receive impulses for future acts through thinking, and experiences repeated Earth lives.

Thus, in human beings there arises a very different necessity for the development and reconfiguration of inherited conditions into an appropriate physical-etheric basis for the individuality: The physical body should become a dwelling place for the spirit. This influence of the spirit, this earthly realization of an individuality, also leads to a different relationship of the seven life processes to body and soul than is the case with animals. In human beings receiving astral influences is not limited to the mere internal presence of the seven life processes, as it is with animals. In human beings, the seven life processes initially serve the formation of the physical organs and their functions and only afterward free themselves from their orientation toward physical formation. The human soul faculties of perception, concentration, interest, and so forth come about because the seven life processes free themselves from being almost exclusively occupied with forming and maintaining physical organs in order to act as soul faculties directed by the spirit. In animals the seven life processes make physical organ activities possible, and therefore also perception, sensation, and movement. At birth, human beings possess the seven life processes in exactly the same way, but the power of the presence of the "I" gradually releases the life processes from their exclusively physical orientation.

In previous chapters, we have described how the gradual anchoring of the seven life processes during the first seven-year-epoch and the resulting development of soul faculties mean quite simply that human beings are fundamentally different from animals because of the presence of their "I"; that includes the etheric constitution as well. By receiving the astral, an animal more or less has the seven life processes inside itself and is therefore a soul-being. Instincts, drives, and desires are thus made possible through the physical organs. In contrast, human children develop much more slowly than animals. A human child does not have the seven life processes immediately present internally, but must painstakingly incorporate them over a period of years. In this way it is possible for the seven life processes to promote the development of soul faculties that subsequently serve the "I."

It is the presence of the "I" that is responsible for the slow development of human beings, but also for the fact that the whole of childhood development serves the free unfolding of the personality. An animal does not go through a metamorphosis in its soul life with the change of teeth, puberty, and adulthood as is the case with a human being. An animal *is* — a human being *will be*! Because a human being is a reincarnating individuality, the inherited physical body, with the help of the etheric body and the seven life processes living within it, is fundamentally transformed in the first seven years of life in order to be able to serve the intentions of the reincarnated individuality. When breathing, warming, nourishing and the other life processes are placed in the service of the incarnating individual, only a regenerating aspect of the life processes remains bound to the physical body. The rest appears in a changed form as soul faculties. The possibility of metamorphosis of the etheric body and thus the release of the life processes from their physical orientation is the result of the presence of the "I." That is what accounts for the slow, consciousness-producing development of human beings. First, it lifts human soul life to a higher level than that of animals by developing the faculties of imagination, thinking, and memory through concentration, interest, and so on; and second, it makes possible metamorphosis of the human soul.

Considered from the viewpoint of the seven life processes, a child's metamorphosis around age seven is the most impressive. Through the presence of the "I" there is the possibility of using individual intentions in transforming the inherited physical body within the first seven years of life so that it can become the best possible physical foundation for the spirit. Thus, it becomes possible that the seven life processes appear more and more as soul faculties after age seven, which, in turn, serve in the unfolding of the personality.

Plants orient themselves to the seven life processes without having internally anchored them. They possess no astral body. *Animals* have the seven life processes more or less anchored internally by way of the physical organs, depending upon their level of development. Animals have an astral body. *Human beings* allow large parts of the seven life processes to be gradually released as soul faculties, which then become soul-enablers of cognition, feelings, and will-driven actions. A human being not only has an astral body, but also an "I" which serves the motives and intentions of the etheric and astral constitutions, as well as the whole development of the individual.

The Seven Life Processes as an Image of Cosmic Effects

Looking back at our efforts to understand the seven life processes, we see how that which is alive in human beings is represented by seven processes that flow through the physical organism, forming, maintaining, and regenerating it. The unceasing overlapping and interaction of these life processes illustrates the constant movement of the etheric in human beings.

However, these movements flow quite freely in and out and all around each other. The individual life processes are less sharply delineated than is the case when observing solid, physical forms. Eyes and ears, bones and muscles, and stomach and intestines all have spatial boundaries; they are clearly separate, physical forms. In contrast, the seven life processes touch each other; no life process is associated exclusively with a specific organ and affecting only that one organ. For instance, breathing, as a life process, does not take place solely in the lungs. There are rhythmic breathing processes in cell respiration, processing of sensory stimuli, peristalsis of the digestive tract, and so on. Secreting is another example. Diffusion of the secreting life process throughout the whole physical organism is not only made apparent in the sorting processes of the intestines, but also in sweat secretion, the releasing of hormones, neurotransmitters, other chemical messengers, and much more. *All* seven life processes pulse through *all* physical formations. As mobile processes they are encountered at all times in every cell of the body.

Besides this, the processes flow over into each other. The effects of breathing in the lungs are given over to the blood, which is distributed throughout the whole organism by a rhythmic pulse to be at the disposal of every single cell in the body. Thus, warming of the organism is dependent upon breathing lungs and a beating heart. However, for their part, they can only develop if the warming life process has already placed a certain amount of warmth at their disposal. Nourishing — taking in substances by way of nutrition, blood, air, or light — can only succeed if accompanied by rhythmic breathing processes and adequate warming of the organs that serve the digestion process. Therefore, even the nourishment functions of the mouth or stomach cannot develop without rhythmic chewing or a certain peristalsis, and also not without a certain body temperature. Counter to this, the lungs cannot breathe and the heart cannot beat unless everything needed to prevent their failure flows to them by way of the processes of nourishing, secreting and maintaining.

Viewed from this perspective, the fact that the life processes "flow in and out and on top of each other" indicates a correlation is to be found between microcosmic human beings and the macrocosmic universe. Viewed from the Earth, there are likewise such moving elements found in the expanses of the cosmos which move among other fixed elements, intersect and cross over one another, and draw their orbits and paths from other fixed formations at varying distances and intensities. These are the planets of our solar system, with different orbits at varying speeds and constantly changing distances from Earth, which move through the constellations of the fixed stars. Breathing, warming, nourishing, and the other life processes move around by way of the eyes, ears, liver, and kidneys just as Saturn, Jupiter and Mars move around the zodiac.

This is, of course, only one correlation between cosmic processes and processes within the human organism. It is thanks to Rudolf Steiner that we are able to understand this correlation in a more profound way. His quest for knowledge was dedicated to understanding the connection of human beings with the surrounding world: "Anthroposophy is a path of knowledge that will lead the spiritual element of human beings to the spiritual element in the cosmic universe" (Steiner, *Anthroposophical Leading Thoughts*, GA 26). On this path of knowledge, the planets are found to be images of the astral sphere and the heaven of fixed stars is found to be an image of the higher spiritual world.

Steiner also indicated that the seven life processes, *breathing, warming, nourishing, secreting, maintaining, growing,* and *reproducing,* although *etheric* processes, have to do with human beings' astrality and have an inner connection with the effects of the spheres of *Saturn, Jupiter, Mars, Sun, Venus, Mercury,* and *Moon;* while out of the higher spiritual world, the fixed, unmoving areas of the twelve senses are formed (Sense of Ego or "I," Sense of Thought, Sense of Speech, Sense of Hearing, Sense of Sight, Sense of Taste, Sense of Smell, Sense of Warmth, Sense of Balance, Sense of Movement, Sense of Life, Sense of Touch).

> *If you correlate this with the twelve areas of the zodiac, what you have is the macro-cosmos; correlate it with the areas of the senses and you have the micro-cosmos. Correlate the seven life processes with the signs of the planets and you have the macro-cosmos and the names of the seven life processes give you the micro-cosmos. The way the movement of the planets in the macro-cosmos behaves in respect to the signs of the zodiac through which they move corresponds with the way the living life processes constantly move and flow through the fixed areas of the senses. So, you see, human beings are, in many respects, a micro-cosmos (Steiner, The Riddle of Humanity, GA 170).*

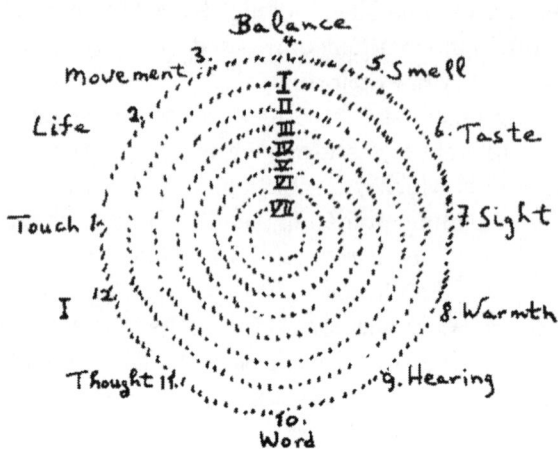

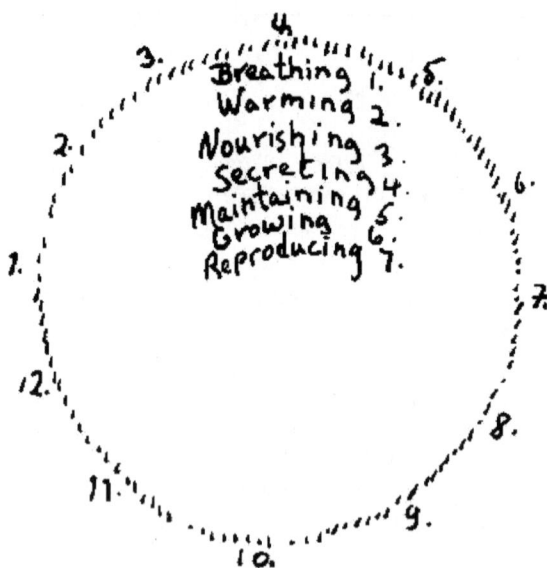

FIGURE 18

The twelve senses and the seven life processes in cosmic connection.

Source: From a blackboard drawing by Rudolf Steiner, The Riddle of Humanity *(GA 170), Lecture 7.*

From these depictions it would be possible to develop a completely new area of sensory-psychology which would have to contain 84 chapters — that is, twelve times seven: going from the breathing, warming, and nourishing processes relating to the sense of smell, all the way to the maintaining, growing, and reproducing processes relating to the sense of hearing. In this way the effects of every single life process as it relates to every single sensory area could be investigated. Because: "The eye lives, the ear lives, that which is the basis for the whole, lives; everything lives. Life dwells in all the senses; it goes throughout all the areas of the senses" (Steiner, *The Riddle of Humanity*, GA 170).

Clarifying these things through exploration is the challenge for anthroposophical education in the home, kindergarten and school. That is the only way one is able to pick up the trail of the physical-etheric basis for learning. In this way, the basic questions of education — "How do people learn? How does a child learn?" — can be expanded through important viewpoints which will lead to deeper understanding from which these questions can be better answered.

Here is a brief indication using the example of the sense of hearing: In order for perception of sound to take place the breathing life process has to be able to develop in the ear — physically, as cell respiration in the relevant regions of the head and, as it relates to the soul, in the form of the ability to perceive a certain sound. Then the warming life process has to be able to develop — physically, in the form of 37°C (98.6°F) temperature surrounding the ear, nerves, and brain and, as it relates to the soul, interest for the sound waves in the air. Now the nourishing life process comes into play — physically, in the form of the ability of sense receptors to receive and then transport via nerve pathways and, as it relates to the soul, an inner connection with that which will be heard. The soul cannot reject it; it must be received by the soul, otherwise one does not hear it! Next comes the secreting life process — physically, in the form of separating and ordering the single frequencies through the structure of the inner ear as well as the release of neurotransmitters by way of synaptic transfers of sensory impressions, and, as it relates to the soul, lifting what has just been heard away from other sounds and sensory impressions. (We can tell that the sound of birds chirping in a tree in the sunshine is coming from the birds and not the sun thanks to the soul-related secreting process.) Next is the maintaining process — physically, it can be observed in the reintegration (re-synthesis) of the previously separated frequency segments, as well as in the synthesis of single tones in the brain to create a unified sound. As it relates to the soul, it has to do with the possibility of remembering something that was heard or associating it with something previously heard. Now the growing life process is added — physically, in the form of growth of the neuronal structure, strengthening synaptic connections as well as training the senses by using them. In relation to the soul, it involves inner growth, improving and perfecting musical understanding. And finally, the producing – reproducing process appears physically in the form of producing the ears, corresponding nerves, and parts of the brain through sound. As it relates to the soul, it involves the ability to imitate sounds, newly create them, or compose something.

This attempt to correlate the life processes with individual senses again makes clear the educational significance of nourishing the seven life processes in general during childhood and youth, but specifically the importance of healthy, strong anchoring of the life processes during the first seven years of life. This anchoring process helps determine how much inner interest and creativity a person brings into learning to manage all areas of life, including music, speech, thinking, and social interaction. In this way, the development of genuine, comprehensive skills and capacities is either promoted or hindered.

> And the further one really goes into consideration of the mysteries of the world, the more one realizes that something like the relationship of twelve to seven is not a gimmick, but that it really does go through all that exists; the fact that it has to be externally expressed through the relationship of the fixed stars to the moving planets is also the result of a part of the great mystery of numbers in world existence. The relationship of the number twelve to the number seven expresses a deep mystery of existence. It expresses the mystery of the human being, as a sensory being, standing in relationship to the life-being; to the self as a life-being. The number twelve contains the mystery of being able to receive an "I." The fact that our senses became twelve — twelve fixed areas — means they are the basis for "I"-consciousness on Earth. The fact that these senses were still life organs during the Moon period is the reason human beings could possess only an astral body; at that time these seven sensory organs were still forming the life organs which were the basis for the astral body. The number seven is the mysterious foundation of the astral body just as the number twelve is the mysterious foundation of the "I"-nature; the human ego (Steiner, The Riddle of Humanity, GA 170).

From these descriptions by Rudolf Steiner, it becomes clearer, once again, why it has to be that plants merely turn to the seven life processes and are internally touched by them instead of taking them into themselves by way of life organs such as lungs, liver, stomach, intestines, or kidneys; they do not have an astral body. And, along with this, it is clear *why* they *cannot* have an astral body. Likewise, it becomes clearer why individual animal species have internalized the various life processes to varying degrees; it depends on the anchoring of the astral body in the animal organism, which has progressed to varying degrees depending on the level of development of individual species.

In *Anthroposophy (A Fragment)* (GA 45), Rudolf Steiner explains in a very sophisticated way how the human physical body, as the carrier of the twelve senses, makes it possible for an "I" to live within it and how the physical body is constructed from forces which are themselves related to the "I." He also explains how a "life-world" forms the life organs in order to *facilitate* "astral human beings." And so the mystery of why the seven life processes of the *etheric* body have something to do with *astrality* is solved. The twelve-part structure of the *physical* senses enables the presence of the "I" and the seven-part structure of the *etheric* life processes enables astrality in human beings.

Steiner's indication that there were only seven living sensory processes during the old Moon period (a previous stage of Earth's development; see Steiner, *The Riddle of Humanity*, GA 170), and not twelve sensory areas as there are today, explains why only now, during the present Earth period, can the "I" be received where previously only an astral body could be received. Lacking were the process of touch, the processes for perceiving an inner sense of life, words, thoughts, and the process for perception of the "I" of another person. These five senses first appeared in the present Earth period, turned the human body into a twelve-fold sensory organism, and enabled the physical incarnation of the "I."

Conclusion

The number twelve, as the number of fixed sensory areas in the human body, related to the "I," and the number seven, as the number of life processes required to make astrality possible in life structures, are facts which have been wisely anchored in human beings from out of spiritual spheres. In order for a child to grow in a healthy way the life processes have to be nourished just as much as the senses.

All education that seeks to develop based on anthroposophy must do so out of an awareness of this fact. The care and training of the twelve senses depends upon the anchoring of the "I" in the human organism, and the colorful complexity of the soul depends upon the care given to the seven life processes. How securely the soul learns to handle its experiences in the world, how it is able to receive with interest and remember that which it encounters through the twelve senses, is conditional upon nourishing the seven life processes.

If these thoughts take root within us like seeds that fall on fertile ground, we may better understand the becoming human being, individually as well as in connection with the challenges of the times, and will allow the art of education to become a living thing. In this regard, we must take seriously Rudolf Steiner's suggestion to not adhere all too strictly to definitions and time schedules, but rather to observe with an inquiring mind and let these things exist in a state of continual, living movement.

This aim of this book has been to provide suggestions about how to improve our understanding of what is living. The seven life processes are only *one* aspect of the etheric. Further aspects will have to be studied in order to expand our grasp of that which lives in human beings.

Appendix

Even though research has been done for many years into the activity of perception, and its role in regard to our lives and learning has often been described, amazingly, many people still think in terms of only five senses.

In her book *Wahrnehmungs- und Bewegungsentfaltung* (Development of Perception and Movement), Paula Tietze-Fritz describes the following areas of the senses:

Touch and Feeling Sense: The sense of contact and pressure is differentiated as the passive part of the sense of touch and haptic (tactile) perception as the active part of the same. Whether or not a child experiences anxiety and mistrust or feelings of security and trust depends upon the many tactile sensory impressions.

The sense of temperature is also located within the organ of the skin.

Visceral perception conveys feelings of love and well-being or lack of well-being through the vegetative nervous system.

Kinesthetic perception conveys the experience of movement within and without through the perception of movement, but is conditional upon the development of the sense of touch.

The vestibular (balance) function perceives our inner ear, conveys spatial positions and our relationship to gravity; our sense of balance.

The sense of smell is referred to as olfactory perception. Tietze-Fritz also relates it to stages of soul development.

The sense of taste is brought into close connection with the sense of touch and smell and its significance for initial experiences of the world is explained.

Visual or optical perception is subtly divided into the categories of perception of color, visual motor coordination (sense of movement), perception of character and motive (sense of speech), consistency of perception (remembering and comparing) and perception of spatial position (sense of balance).

Auditory or acoustic perception depends purely upon hearing noises, sounds, voices and tones together, but the significance of movement, the sense of balance as well as the perception of touch as a previous development is clearly explained. The connection between remembering and the capability of character-motive perception in association with speech development is described. The author classifies vibratory perception with acoustic perception.

Just like Steiner, Montessori, Piaget, Hengstenberg, Ayres, Affolter, Frostig, Hellbruegge and many others, Paula Tietze-Fritz clearly explains the connection between developing perceptual capability, physical health and learning ability. Knowledge about the multiplicity of the senses has long existed. Unfortunately this knowledge is still not often applied in the field of learning processes.

Bibliography

A NOTE ON THE CITATIONS
In general, author and year are cited in the main text. If an English edition of the book is available, the year of that edition is cited.

With works by Rudolf Steiner (written works and lectures), the GA number is given in order to identify the specific source within the list of collected works (gesamtausgabe) in German. If the text is available in English, the English title is included. However, please note that all excerpts have been freshly translated for this volume rather than reproduced from the English editions.

Works by Steiner are listed below in order of their GA number.

* * *

Jennifer Ackerman, *Sex, Sleep, Eat, Drink, Dream: A Day in the Life of your Body*, Mariner Books, 2008.

Aaron Antonovsky, *Salutogenese. Zur Entmystifizierung der Gesundheit*, Tübingen, 1997. (Salutogenesis: Unraveling the Mystery of Health)

Jörg Blech, *Gene sind kein Schicksal. Wie wir unsere Erbanlagen und unser Leben steuern können*, Frankfurt, 2010. (Genes Are Not Destiny. How We Can Guide Our Own Life and Hereditary Disposition)

Mark Buchta, Dirk W. Höper and Andreas Sönnichsen (Eds.), *Das Hammerexamen. Repetitorium für den 2. Abschnitt der Aerztlichen Pruefung*, Munich, 2006. (Hammer Exams. Revision Course for the Second Part of the Medical Certification Exam)

Erwin Bünning, *Die physiologische Uhr. Circadiane Rhythmik und Biochronometrie*, Berlin, 1977. (The Physiological Clock: Circadian Rhythm and Biochronometry)

Neil A. Campbell and Jane B. Reece, *Biologie*, Heidelberg/Berlin, 1997. (Biology)

Adolf Faller, *Der Körper des Menschen. Einführung in Bau und Funktion*, Stuttgart, 1999. (The Human Body; Introduction to Form and Function) Available in English as *The Human Body: An Introduction to Structure and Function*, Thieme, Stuttgart, 2004.

Michael Feld, *Das dunkle Kapitel unserer Arbeitswelt*, in *FAZ*, 12/10/2008, Issue #289, p. N1. (The Dark Chapter in Our World of Employment)

Thomas Fuchs, *Das Gehirn – ein Beziehungsorgan. Eine phaenomenologisch-oekologische Konzeption*, Stuttgart, 2010. (The Brain: A Relationship Organ: A Phenomenological-Ecological Conception)

Karl Gebauer and Gerald Hüther, *Kinder brauchen Vertrauen, Erfolgreiches Lernen durch starke Beziehungen*, Zürich, 2004. (Children Need Trust: Successful Learning Through Strong Relationships)

Philipp Gelitz, *Chronobiologie in der pädagogischen Praxis*, in: *Erziehungskunst* 1/2009. (Chronobiology in Educational Practice)

Michaela Glöckler (Ed.), *Gesundheit und Schule. Schulärztliche Tätigkeit an Waldorf- und Rudolf Steiner Schulen. Berufsbild – Perspektiven – praktische Erfahrungen. Erziehung als präventiv-medizinische Aufgabenstellung*, Dornach, 1998. (Health and School)

Gunther Hildebrandt, *Biologische Rhythmen und Arbeit. Bausteine zur Chronobiologie und Chronohygiene der Arbeitsgestaltung*, Berlin, 1976. (Biological Rhythms and Work)

Walter Holtzapfel, *Im Kraftfeld der Organe. Leber, Lunge, Niere, Herz*, Dornach, 2004. Available in English as *The Human Organs: Their Functional and Psychological Significance: Liver, Lung, Kidney, Heart*, Floris Books, 2014.

Coenraad van Houten, *Erwachsenenbildung als Willenserweckung*, Stuttgart, 1999. Available in English as *Awakening the Will: Principles and Processes in Adult Education*, Forest Row, 1999.

Friedrich Husemann and Otto Wolf, *Das Bild des Menschen als Grundlage der Heilkunst, Volume I: Zur Anatomie und Physiologie*, Stuttgart, 2003. (The Image of the Human Being as the Foundation of Healing: Anatomy and Physiology)

Klaus D. Jürgens, ed., *Physiologie, Lehrbuch der Funktionen des menschlichen Koerpers*, Munich, 2004. (Physiology: Textbook of the Functions of the Human Body)

Rainer Klinke and Stefan Silbernagel, *Lehrbuch der Physiologie*, Stuttgart, 1996. (Physiology Textbook)

Karl König, *Der Kreis der Zwölf Sinne und die sieben Lebensprozesse*, Stuttgart 1999. (The Circle of the Twelve Senses and the Seven Life Processes) Available in English as *A Living Physiology*, Camphill Foundation, 1999.

Olaf Koob, *Wenn die Organe sprechen könnten. Grundlagen der leiblich-seelischen Gesundheit*, Stuttgart, 2005. (If Organs Could Speak: Basis for the Health of Body and Soul)

Ernst-Michael Kranich, *Anthropologische Grundlagen der Waldorf-pädagogik*, Stuttgart, 1999. (Anthropological Foundations of Waldorf Education)

Clemens Kuby, *Heilung, das Wunder in uns. Selbstheilungsprozesse entdecken*, München, 2005. (Healing; the Miracle in Us; Discover Self-Healing Processes)

Petra Kühne, *Säuglingsernährung. Stillen und vegetarische Beikost*, Unterlengenhardt, 2004. (Nutrition for Infants: Breastfeeding and Vegetarian Solid Foods)

Konrad Kunsch and Steffen Kunsch, *Der Mensch in Zahlen. Eine Datensammlung in Tabellen mit über 20.000 Einzelwerten*, Heidelberg, 2006. (Humanity by the Numbers: A Collection of Data Tables with over 20,000 Entries)

Bernard Lievegoed, *Entwicklungsphasen des Kindes,* Stuttgart, 1982. (Children's Developmental Phases). Available in English as *Phases of Childhood*, Floris, revised edition 2005.

Christof Lindenau, *Der übende Mensch, Anthroposophie-Studium als Ausgangspunkt moderner Geistesschulung,* Stuttgart, 1981. (Human Being in Training, The Study of Anthroposophy as a Starting Point for Modern Spiritual Training)

Christoph Lindenberg (ed.), *Rudolf Steiner, Zur Sinneslehre, Acht Vorträge,* Stuttgart 2004. (The Twelve Senses - Eight Lectures)

Pim van Lommel, *Endloses Bewusstein. Neue medizinische Fakten zur Nahtoderfahrung,* Eschbach, 2011. (Endless Consciousness; New Medical Facts about Near-Death Experience) Available in English as *Consciousness Beyond Life: The Science of the Near-Death Experience,* HarperCollins, 2011.

Ernst Marti, *Die vier Aether. Zu Rudolf Steiners Aetherlehre,* Stuttgart, 2010. Available in English as *The Four Ethers: Contributions to Rudolf Steiner's science of the ethers,* Schaumburg Publications, 1984.

Frank H. Netter, *Atlas der Anatomie des Menschen,* Munich 2008. Available in English as *Atlas of Human Anatomy,* sixth edition, Elsevier Health Services, 2014.

Hermann Pfrogner, *Die sieben Lebensprozesse, Eine musiktherapeutische Anregung,* Freiburg, 1978. (The Seven Life Processes, Suggestions for Music Therapy)

Benita Quadflieg-von Vegesack, *Ungewöhnliche Kleinkinder and ihre heilpädagogische Förderung,* Ostfildern, 1998. (Exceptional Young Children and their Advancement through Curative Education)

Heinrich Reichert, *Neurobiologie,* Stuttgart and New York, 2000. (Neurobiology)

Herbert Renz-Polster and Steffen Krautzig, *Basislehrbuch Innere Medizin,* Munich, 2008. (Basic Textbook for Internal Medicine)

Johannes W. Rohen, *Morphologie des menschlichen Organismus. Eine goetheanistische Gestaltlehre des Menschen,* Stuttgart 2007. (Morphology of the Human Organism) Available in English as *Functional Morphology, the Dynamic Wholeness of the Human Organism,* Adonis Press, 2007.

Bernd Rosslenbroich, *Die rhythmische Organisation des Menschen,* Stuttgart, 1994. (The Rhythmic Organization of the Human Being)

Johann Caspar Rüegg, *Gehirn, Psyche und Körper. Neurobiologie von Psychosomatik und Psychotherapie*, Stuttgart, 2007. (Brain, Psyche and Body; Neurobiology of Psychosomatic and Psychotherapy)

Wolfgang Schad, *Die Zeitordnung des Menschen und ihre pädagogische Bedeutung*, in *Erziehungskunst* 5/1994. (Human Organization of Time and Its Significance for Education)

Robert F. Schmidt and Florian Lang, *Physiologie des Menschen*, Berlin/ Heidelberg 2007. (Human Physiology)

Robert F. Schmidt & Gerhard Thews, *Physiologie des Menschen*, Berlin 1985. (Human Physiology)

Hubert Schneemann and Gisela Wurm (Eds.), *Hagers Handbuch der pharmazeutischen Praxis. Folgeband 1: Waren und Dienste*, Berlin 1995. (Hager's Handbook of Pharmaceutical Practice, Supplementary Volume 1)

Albert Soesman, *Die zwölf Sinne – Tore der Seele,* Stuttgart, 2009. (The Twelve Senses – Doors of the Soul) Available in English as *Our Twelve Senses: How Healthy Senses Refresh the Soul*, Hawthorn Press, 2001.

Rudolf Steiner, GA 9. *Theosophie.* Originally published as a book, 1904. Available in English as *Theosophy*, SteinerBooks, 1994.

Rudolf Steiner, GA 15. *Die geistige Führung des Menschen und der Menschheit.* Three lectures given in 1910, reworked as a book, 1911. Available in English as *The Spiritual Guidance of the Individual and Humanity*, SteinerBooks, 1992.

Rudolf Steiner, GA 24. *Aufsätze über die Dreigliederung des sozialen Organismus und zur Zeitlage 1915-1921.* (Essays Concerning the Tripartite Division of the Social Organism and the Time Period 1915-1921) Essays and articles originally published in various periodicals and gathered in book form in 1921.

Rudolf Steiner, GA 26. *Anthroposophische Leitsätze, Der Erkenntnisweg der Anthroposophie—Das Michael-Mysterium.* Material originally circulated to members of the Anthroposophical Society, first published in book form in 1924. Available in English as *Anthroposophical Leading Thoughts*, Rudolf Steiner Press, 1973.

Rudolf Steiner, GA 34. *Die Erziehung des Kindes vom Gesichtspunkte der Geisteswissenschaft* (The Education of the Child from the Viewpoint of Spiritual Science). Essay from the magazine *Luzifer–Gnosis*, originally published in 1909. Available in English in *The Education of the Child and Early Lectures on Education*, SteinerBooks, 1996.

Rudolf Steiner, GA 36. *Der Goetheanumgedanke inmitten der Kulturkrisis der Gegenwart, Gesammelte Aufsätze aus der Wochenschrift "Das Goetheanum" 1921–1925* (Goethean Thought in the Midst of the Present Cultural Crisis, Essays from the Newsletter *Das Goetheanum*, 1921–1925).

Rudolf Steiner, GA 45. *Anthroposophie: Ein Fragment aus dem Jahre 1910.* Available in English as *Anthroposophy (A Fragment)*, SteinerBooks, 1996.

Rudolf Steiner, GA 128. *Eine okkulte Physiologie.* Eight lectures given in Prague, 1911. Available in English as *An Occult Physiology,* Rudolf Steiner Press, 1997.

Rudolf Steiner, GA 170. *Das Rätsel des Menschen. Die geistigen Hintergründe der menschlichen Geschichte. Kosmische und Menschliche Geschichte Band I* (The Riddle of Man. The spiritual background of human history. Cosmic and Human History Volume I). Fifteen lectures given in Dornach, 1916. Available in English as *The Riddle of Humanity*, Rudolf Steiner Press, 1990.

Rudolf Steiner, GA 218. *Geistige Zusammenhänge in der Gestaltung des menschlichen Organismus* (Spiritual Relationships in the Forming of the Human Body). Lectures given in various cities, 1922. Some lectures found in *Waldorf Education and Anthroposophy, Volume 2*, SteinerBooks, 1996.

Rudolf Steiner, GA 224. *Die menschlichen Seele in ihrem Zusammenhang mit göttlich-geistigen Individualitaeten. Die Verinnerlichung der Jahresfeste* (The Human Soul in Its Relationship with Divine-Spiritual Individualities; Internalization of the Yearly Festivals). Lectures given in various cities, 1923.

Rudolf Steiner, GA 230. *Der Mensch als Zusammenklang des schaffenden, bildenden und gestaltenden Weltenwortes* (The Human Being as Harmony of the Creating, Forming, and Shaping World Word). Twelve lectures given in Dornach, 1923. Available in English as *Harmony of the Creative Word*, Rudolf Steiner Press, 2002.

Rudolf Steiner, GA 266. *Aus den Inhalten der esoterischen Stunden, Gedächtnisaufzeichnungen von Teilnehmern. Band 1, 1904–1909.* (From the Contents of the Esoteric Lessons, Lecture Notes from Participants) Available in English as *Esoteric Lessons Part I: 1904–1909*, Steiner-Books, 2011.

Rudolf Steiner, GA 293. *Allgemeine Menschenkunde als Grundlage der Pädagogik* (The Study of Man as the Basis of Education). 14 lectures given in Stuttgart, 1919. Available in English as *Study of Man*, translated by A C Harwood, Rudolf Steiner Press, London, 1995 and also as *The Foundations of Human Experience*, SteinerBooks, 1996.

Rudolf Steiner, GA 303. *Die Gesunde Entwicklung des Menschenwesens. Eine Einführung in die Anthroposophische Pädagogik und Didaktik* (The Healthy Development of the Human Being. An Introduction to Anthroposophic Pedagogy). 16 lectures given in Dornach, 1921–1922. Available in English as *Soul Economy: Body, Mind, and Spirit in Waldorf Education*, SteinerBooks, 2003.

Rudolf Steiner, GA 304a. *Anthroposophische Menschenkunde und Pädagogik* (Anthroposophical Study of Man and Education). Available in English in *Waldorf Education and Anthroposophy, Volumes 1 and 2*, SteinerBooks, 1995 and 1996

Rudolf Steiner, GA 306. *Die pädagogische Praxis vom Gesichtspunkte geisteswissenschaftlicher Menschenerkenntnis.* 8 lectures given in Dornach, 1923. Available in English as *The Child's Changing Consciousness as the Basis of Pedagogical Practice*, SteinerBooks, 1996.

Rudolf Steiner, GA 310. *Der pädagogische Wert der Menschenerkenntnis und der Kulturwert der Pädagogik* (The Pedagogical Value of Human Knowledge and Cultural Value of Education). 10 lectures given in Arnheim, 1924. Available in English as *Human Values in Education*, SteinerBooks, 2002.

Rudolf Steiner, GA 313. *Geisteswissenschaftliche Gesichtspunkte zur Therapie* (Spiritual-Scientific Aspects of Therapy). 9 lectures given in Dornach, 1921. Available in English as *Illness and Therapy: Spiritual-Scientific Aspects of Healing*, SteinerBooks.

Rudolf Steiner, GA 316. *Meditative Betrachtungen und Anleitungen zur Vertiefung der Heilkunst* (Meditative Considerations and Instructions for Deepening the Art of Healing). 14 lectures given in Dornach, 1924. Available in English as *Course for Young Doctors*, Mercury Press, 1994, and as *Understanding Healing*, Rudolf Steiner Press, 2014.

Rudolf Steiner, GA 317. *Heilpädagogischer Kurs* (Curative Education Course). 12 lectures given in Dornach, 1924. Available in English as *Education for Special Needs*, Rudolf Steiner Press, 2015.

Rudolf Steiner, GA 327. *Geisteswissenschaftliche Grundlagen zum Gedeihen der Landwirtschaft. Landwirtschaftlicher Kursus* (Spiritual-Scientific Foundations of Agriculture. The Agriculture Course). 8 lectures given in Koberwitz, 1924. Available in English as *The Agriculture Course*, Biodynamic Association, 1974.

Rudolf Steiner, GA 343. *Vorträge und Kurse über christlich-religiöses Wirken. II: Spirituelles Erkennen – Religiöses Empfinden – Kultisches Handeln* (Lectures and Courses about Christian-Religious Works; II: Spiritual Perception – Religious Feeling – Sacred Action). 29 lectures given in Dornach, 1921.

Rudolf Steiner, GA 351. *Mensch und Welt. Das Wirken des Geistes in der Natur. Über das Wesen der Bienen* (Man and World. The Working of the Spirit in Nature. On the Life of the Bee). 12 lectures given in Dornach, 1921. Some lectures found in English in *Bees*, SteinerBooks, 1998.

Rudolf Steiner, GA 354. *Die Schöpfung der Welt und des Menschen. Erdenleben und Sternenwirken* (The Creation of the World and of The Human Being. Earthly Life and the Workings of the Stars). 14 lectures given in Dornach, 1924. Available in English as *From Sunspots to Strawberries*, Rudolf Steiner Press, 2002.

Paula Tietze-Fritz, *Wahrnehmungs- und Bewegungsentfaltung. Heilpädagogische Förderung des Kindes in seinen ersten 24 Monaten*, Heidelberg, 1982. (Development of Perception and Movement: Curative Education Challenges in the First 24 Months)

Michael Werner and Thomas Stöckli, *Life from Light: Is it possible to live without food? A scientist reports on his experiences*, Clairview Books Ltd, 2012.

About the Authors

PHILIPP GELITZ was born in 1981 and has a daughter. He is a state-certified teacher and Waldorf teacher who works at the full-day kindergarten at the Kassel Waldorf School in Germany. He publishes regularly in the German-language magazine *Erziehungskunst* (The Art of Education) on subjects dealing with early childhood.

ALMUTH STREHLOW was born in 1959 and has three children. She is a teacher with additional training in psychomotor learning and art therapy. She also has a master's degree in continuing education, adult education and school management. Since 1992 she has been a lecturer at the Rudolf Steiner Institute in Kassel, Germany. She gives seminars and lectures in Germany and abroad.

Other WECAN books you will enjoy:

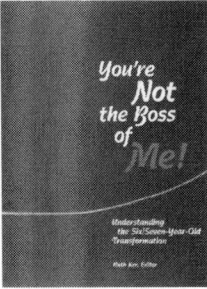

You're Not the Boss of Me!
Understanding the Six/Seven-Year-Old Transformation
Edited by Ruth Ker

A treasury of guidance and inspiration for working with children at the threshold of the six/seven-year change. **$32**

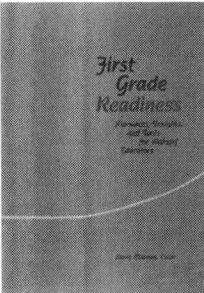

First Grade Readiness
Resources, Insights and Tools for Waldorf Educators
Edited by Nancy Blanning

Essential research and resources for anyone involved in making first grade readiness decisions. **$25**

Cradle of a Healthy Life
Early Childhood and the Whole of Life
Nine WECAN Conference Lectures by Dr. Johanna Steegmans, with summaries of lectures by Dr. Gerald Karnow

This volume collects the valuable contributions of two medical doctors to recent WECAN conferences. **$14**

Other WECAN books you will enjoy:

Made in the USA
Middletown, DE
08 December 2024

65882283R00102